SEARCH ENGINE O

SEO

HOW TO OPTIMIZE YOUR WEB SITE FOR INTERNET SEARCH ENGINES

GOOGLE, YAHOO!, MSN LIVE, AOL, ASK, ALTAVISTA, FAST, GIGABLAST, SNAP, LOOKSMART, AND MORE

Samuel Blankson

Published by Blankson Enterprises Ltd.,
www.practicalbooks.org. Print on demand publishing made
available through Lighting Source UK.

A copy of this title is held by the British Library.

Paperback Edition (9x6)
ISBN 10: 1-9057-8906-8
ISBN 13: 978-1-905-789-06-1

Hardback Edition (9x6)
ISBN 10:1-9057-8907-6
ISBN 13: 978-1-905-789-07-8

EBook Edition
ISBN 10: 1-9057-8921-1
ISBN 13: 978-1-905-789-21-4

Acknowledgements

Special thanks to all those who contributed to the creation of this book, in particular a special thank you is extended to:

MANAGING EDITOR
SHANNON D. MELCHER
(authorright.com)

PRE-EDITOR
LILI BOOTH

COVER DESIGN
SONA & JACOB
(sonaandjacob.com)

**RESEARCH &
CONTRIBUTING EDITOR**
JUDY COLE

INDEXERS
JUDY COLE
JENNIFER D. MELCHER

About the Author

Samuel Blankson is an avid reader, author, poet, songwriter, photographer, athlete, programmer, traveler, researcher and securities trader. He has authored over thirty books on a wide range of subjects: *META Tags—Optimising Your Website for Internet Search Engines, The Guide to IT Contracting, The Kolumbas Affair, Living the Ultimate Truth*-1st and 2nd edition, are some of his works.

He has also authored children's books, fiction novels, self-empowerment books and a multitude of calendars. Having written over 100 songs, sixty of which are featured in *Sixty Original Song Lyrics*, Mr. Blankson continues to expand his horizons by blending his creativity with his passion and business acumen.

A short biography of Samuel Blankson can be found at www.samuelblankson.com and his books may be purchased from www.practicalbooks.org.

Contents

Dedication

*To God, for blessing me
with all I have.
To my wife, Uju,
for regularly
reminding me
of God's work.*

From the Author

In the last eight years I have set up Web sites to promote, market and sell the various products and literature that I produce. In doing so, I have learned through time consuming, expensive and painful trial and error, many of the lessons covered in this book.

During this period, while I have stumbled upon small pockets of useful information from a multitude of sources, both online and offline, I have found it a challenge, and at times nearly impossible, to find one source for all the information that a Web site operator requires to improve his or her chances of being discovered, visited and revisited by Internet users.

While there are many books on corporate Web marketing, few good sources exist to help the owners of small Web sites and businesses who cannot afford the armies of Web developers, designers, traffic analysts, marketers and content creators, often needed to realize any measurable success in the endeavor.

If, like me, you run your own Web business or manage your own Web site and virtually have to undertake all these roles yourself, then you will appreciate what this book offers—a single source for all search engine optimization (SEO) information that you will need to know to succeed online.

I have kept the tone and pace of this book casual and easy to read, unlike corporate Web marketing manuals, which tend to be rigid, highly technical and formal. Wherever possible, I have given links to sources for services or information, thus freeing this book from clutter and mountains of indistinct reference information.

This book can be read by anyone, whether you are just starting out with your own Web site, or even if you have been running many Web sites for a while. I have tried to keep the jargon to a minimum, while explaining the fundamental concepts and giving practical advice and information to enable you to immediately apply the methodologies covered in this book.

Divided into five sections, this book covers each major SEO subject. The first chapter is an introduction to the Internet, Web sites and the variables associated with SEO, including search engines and the differing types of Web searches.

The second chapter delves deeper into Web site optimization for search engines: It covers META tags, search engine and directory submissions, back-links, banner exchanges and other related topics.

The third chapter covers social marketing and how to utilize these resources. Groups, forums, really simple syndication (RSS) and blogging are some of the many social topics covered in this chapter.

The fourth chapter deals with a topic that most Web masters will be very interested in and that you will need to know as well—driving Internet sales traffic to your Web site. Chapter four covers paid inclusion(s), banner advertising, affiliate marketing and other related topics.

The fifth chapter focuses on the monitoring tools and how to fine-tune your marketing campaigns. Chapter five discusses Google's Adwords, Analytics and Webmaster Tools in great detail.

Finally, the sixth chapter covers offline methods of promoting your Web site. The use of news and PR releases, books, seminars, billboards, radio, television and other conventional advertising resources are thoroughly discussed. A host of helpful resources on all topics are also given.

Many factors will determine your Web site's marketability and success; such as its design, content, niche or topic, service, products, competition, domain name, etc. However, this book will give your Web site the best advantage of getting ahead (and staying ahead), no matter what you have begun with and regardless of your current level of expertise.

Samuel Blankson

Introduction

If you own a Web site, or are thinking of operating your business over the Internet, promoting a service or product, or even generating interest and awareness of a brand, idea or information source, you will quickly become aware of the difficulties involved with gaining attention and attracting Web visitors.

People who use the Internet are either looking for information, entertainment, communication, or a product or service (and may or may not be prepared to pay for it). We will examine ways to get Internet users to visit your Web site, or relevant pages.

While the Internet is a phenomenal resource for data, information, knowledge and marketing of products and services, you can easily get lost among the countless billions of Web sites currently offering these resources. To stand out and be noticed among the competition will require the application of specific promotional and marketing techniques.

We will thus examine how people use the Internet, what they look for, how they find it and what makes them return to your site. We will also look at how to build awareness of your Web presence, drive traffic (visitors) to your site, generate interest in your site's content, and the offline promotional options available to you.

Unlike offline marketing which can be expensive for a Web site owner, Internet marketing techniques are either free or relatively inexpensive when compared to offline marketing options.

One of the problems of any marketing plan is the measurement of effectiveness. The effect of applying online marketing techniques tends to be more immediate and easier to measure than offline promotions. For each technique covered throughout this book we will examine the related topics of how to measure the results.

If you are new to Internet marketing, your journey through this book will introduce you to many new procedures. While you do not need to be highly skilled at Web technologies to use this book, you will need access to the Internet and be familiar with the details of the preceding book in this series, "*META Tags: Optimizing Your Web site for Internet Search Engines. ISBN-10: 190578998X, ISBN-13: 978-1905789986* (Blankson, 2007)".

Some techniques in this book will have associated risks of being banned by search engines or Internet service providers. Wherever these risks exist, they will be highlighted near the introduction of the technique. This book is a thorough coverage of the subject matter and is intended to be used in a legal manner.

However, you should be aware that some techniques may either be frowned upon or illegal in certain countries. These risks will also be highlighted throughout the book; it is your responsibility to ensure that you are conforming to all Internet usage laws and rules in your jurisdiction. **It is not intended for you to use any technique or information in this book to break any laws.**

Please Note: Unless otherwise specified, all Web site addresses (URLs), are preceded by (http://).

Chapter 1

Internet, Web Sites & Search Engines

Internet

Around the late 1950's and early 1960's, the need for separate computer networks to connect and communicate with each other led to the research and development of the technologies that gave birth to the Internet today. The Internet is simply that: a growing group of computer networks and individual computer systems which communicate with each other through a standard electronic language.

This has formed a World Wide Web of interconnected computer networks. You and I access this World Wide Web through a node or an Internet Services Provider (ISP). Your ISP may head one of the networks connected directly to the Internet, or it may be part of a larger network of other ISPs that form a network that is a node on the Internet.

Organizations sprung up and standards were quickly developed to allow more systems to be incorporated into this World Wide Web of interconnected computer systems. These standards dealt with everything from text messaging, e-mail, searching, Web sites and Web pages, security, privacy and many more topics that have become integrated and almost invisible to the Internet users of today.

Web Browsers

Perhaps the most important addition to the toolset developed by the Internet pioneers was the Web browser This tool has quickly grown to be the tool of choice for almost every Internet user. It is through the Internet browser that most Internet users experience the World Wide Web. Today, Microsoft's Internet Explorer, Mozilla Foundation's Firefox and Opera Software Company's Opera Internet browser software applications are examples of popular Web browsers.

Through these Web browsers, Web sites and Web pages come alive. To access a Web site you must first have access to the Internet through an ISP. Similarly, you must also have a computer connected to an Internet access point. Today this could be through a dialup telephone line, ISDN phone line, cable or other digital subscriber line (DSL) connection, across your phone line, a leased line, local area network (LAN) or through a wireless connection.

Searching

However you choose to connect to the Internet, your computer must have an Internet browser to view the Web pages of any Web site. To find the Web site you are looking for, you will either need to know its address, e.g., www.practicalbooks.org, or you can search for the site using an Internet search engine. Google, Yahoo!, MSN Live, AOL, Ask, AltaVista, FAST, GigaBlast, Snap and LookSmart are the major players in this field.

All these search engines provide their services via their Web sites, i.e., www.alltheweb.com, www.yahoo.com, www .msn.com, www.altavista.com, www.google.com, www.aol .com, etc. Most of these search engines also provide access to their search facilities through local or regional Web sites. For instance, the UK Yahoo! can be found at www.yahoo.co.uk. Similarly the Japanese Google can be found at www.google.jp. These regional sites provide language and region specific search results (most of the time).

Web Sites and Web Pages

A Web site is composed of all the files encapsulated within a Web domain, e.g., www.practicalbooks.org. For instance, all Web pages, databases, scripts, and data files – hidden or visible to Web users – within practicalbooks.org, make up the www.practicalbooks.org Web site. Web sites can link to other Web pages within other Web sites. This can give a Web site access to other Web sites' information, products or services. For instance, your Web site's product order page may access an e-commerce provider's services such as PayPal's, or your Web pages could display news generated by CNN, BBC or Reuters.

Web pages are written as lines of code in HyperText Markup Language (HTML). This code represents the graphical Web pages you will see on the Internet. HTML is limited in how it can be used to display interactive moving images; therefore scripts which HTML encapsulates have been developed to bridge some of these limitations. JavaScript is one such scripting language. Web browsers must be java enabled to enable JavaScript features to function.

Web Page Format

At the beginning of all Web pages is the declaration of what the pages is about, what it will allow and what it will not allow. These declarations are called META Tags. *"META Tags: Optimizing Your Website for Internet Search Engines. ISBN-10: 190578998X, ISBN-13: 978-1905789986"*, covers these tags in great detail. Part of every SEO exercise should include optimizing your Web page's META Tags.

The declaration portion of the Web page remains "invisible" in the graphical page displayed by the Web browser. However, the Web browser uses the declaration details to determine how the page should be displayed and treated. After the declaration of the page type, META Tags, and scripts, the body of your Web page begins. Within this body, the "visible" page content and behavior are specified.

In a sense, all SEO involves getting Web users who are interested in your Web page's content, to find your Web page among the numerous competing Web pages. More numerous than the Web pages available on the World Wide Web, are the Web users. Accessing the Internet from all parts of the globe are millions of people and computer programs called robots, all seeking information, products and/or services from Web pages and Web sites.

The robots are mainly used by search engines and some Web sites, to "mine" or "crawl" for data through the pages on the World Wide Web, and through some private networks. For the Internet search engines, this is one of the ways they gather information about what is out there on the World Wide Web. By crawling through Web pages that allow them, these robots help search engines create a clearer index, model or map of the Internet data space. This helps search engines find relevant information faster when you execute a search request.

Web Traffic

On the Internet, your Web traffic is determined by how many people access your Web site or Web page. While traffic is great and we all want more of it, relevancy is more important than volume alone when it comes to sales.

A Web site that receives 200 hits per month (visits by Web users to a Web site) and achieves 100 sales from this traffic is better than a site that receives 100,000 hits a month and only achieves 100 sales. The former example implies more relevant traffic visits than the latter. Work may be needed to improve the traffic volume for the former example, while additional effort may be necessary to improve the relevancy of the site content, and SEO campaign for the latter.

In the previous examples we spoke of improving sales; however, not all Web traffic is looking to buy. In fact, the majority of Web traffic is looking to find information, while the minority is actually shopping.

Information Seekers

The vast majority of Internet users are looking for information or casually passing time. Generally, people are reading e-mail, news articles, chatting to friends, socializing through social Web sites such as www.myspace.com or playing games, watching movie previews, or clips on www.youtube.com, while others are listening to music or Web radio broadcasts.

These Internet users may not be currently looking to purchase a service or a product; however, a small percentage of them can be convinced to buy, if you offer them enticing information while building a desire within them for your product or service. We will look at this and other ways to convert information seekers into buyers later. However, for now you can assume that any Internet user not looking for premium information or a product to purchase, is in the information seeker category.

Researchers

Researchers, teachers, students and other Internet users seeking answers to their questions often go to research Web sites. These sites, such as www.wiki.com, among many others, offer vast amounts of information for free. They are excellent informational resources. Because the information is so easily available, and very often offered for free, it is difficult to entice these Internet users to focus on buying your product or service. This is especially true if your product or service will not help them further their research.

There are, however, uses for Internet users in this category. Acquiring their names and contact details, i.e., e-mail addresses and their shopping preferences, is one such use. We shall look at how site membership and a short survey preceding the provision of research information is one of the best ways to utilize researcher traffic. If you want to attract this type of traffic, your Web site has to have in-depth information on the topic of the Web site and its Web pages.

Buyers

Buyers are perhaps the best type of Internet user a Web site owner can have. These Web users are actually looking to buy something. You simply have to attract them to your site and if the price and terms are favorable to them, the sale is virtually in the bag. DVD's, books, music, auction items, training courses, travel packages, flights, office stationary, computer parts and sales, utility services, insurance, clothing, grocery shopping, and virtually anything that can be sold, is currently being offered by someone on the Internet.

To attract this traffic, you need to be indexed by the major search engines and be popular. This means your Web site content and SEO must be highly relevant to the buyers interested in your product or service. There are many ways of achieving relevancy to buyers; beginning with optimization of your Web site and Web pages, which will allow search engines to find you and then consider your Web pages to be the most relevant, for the most popular search keywords used by buyers of your product or service.

Search Engines

Search engines allow Internet users to search for information by providing keywords or a search phrase. The search engine then matches the most relevant Web pages in its directory or index with the search keywords or keyword phrase. Today's top search engines are either search directories, or they use crawlers (Web robots) to create an index of Web sites. Crawlers also normally offer a free or paid submission service.

Search Directories

Directories are search engines where the Web site or Web page listings are added by human beings similar to a telephone directory. They normally charge Web site administrators, (Web masters) for inclusion in the directory. A few of them offer free inclusion in the directory, while nowadays, the trend is fast moving towards paid inclusion. Examples of search directories are www.yahoo.com, www.dmoz.com and www.msn.com. Some of these directories such as Yahoo! and MSN also use Web crawlers.

Crawlers

Crawlers are search engines that use Web crawlers. Web crawlers are small automated scripts also called Web robots or Web spiders; to "spider" or methodically browse the Internet and download Web pages, or portions of Web pages, for search engines. The contents of these downloaded Web pages are later indexed which allows crawler search engines to quickly produce search results, matching the searches to the index, rather than the actual Internet Web page's content.

Popular crawler search engines including Google, Yahoo!, and Microsoft Live also offer a way for Web masters to pay to submit their Web sites. Because these sites are crawlers, even if you do not pay to be submitted, your site will eventually be indexed by the search robots and included in the search engine index. However, if you want to get your Web site indexed faster, paying can normally get you included within two days.

Paid Listings

Some search engines also offer another type of service that allows you to artificially improve your search placements. This is called pay-per-click or paid listing. LookSmart, Google and www.overture.com (now owned by Yahoo! and called Yahoo! Search Marketing), all offer services where you can pay to be listed in the top of your chosen keyword's searches. Google AdWords is a pay-per-click service as is Overture's and LookSmart's paid listing services.

Overture used to be solely a paid listing provider. However, now that it is part of Yahoo!, it will be more like Google, which both offer free search facilities as well as selling their listings to other search engines. Google does this with AOL, while Yahoo! Search Marketing does this to Yahoo!, AltaVista, MSN, Lycos, and Ask (also fed by LookSmart).

Search Engine Results Page (SERP)

When an Internet user executes a search on a search engine, the results are displayed on a SERP. The major search engines' SERPs may include contextual searches where keywords are used to match concepts, rather than keywords on Web pages, algorithmic, or organic listings (where keywords are used to search indexes created with Web robots or human maintained directories). The SERP could also include suggested search refinements in the form of "Did you mean…?", spelling suggestions, images, maps, books, music, groups, blogs and many other search refinement suggestions.

Search listings normally include non-sponsored search listings as the main part of the SERP. Sponsored listings with descriptions are ususally at the top or to the right side of the SERP, and sometimes at the bottom, but normally without descriptive text as currently used by Yahoo!. The search engines make the vast majority of their revenue from sponsored links and will try to cram as much on a SERP as they can get away with, without detracting from the user's search experience.

Types of Searches

All major search engines also offer different types of searches such as images, news, maps and video, with many others also offering searches for shopping, audio and music, books, blogs, groups, University and scholarly reports and papers, Yellow Page listings and local resources. The types of SERPs for these specialized searches may also offer added functionality and features.

Search Engine Market Share

How each search engine determines relevance for searches is a closely guarded secret. However, through reverse engineering the SEO community has unlocked the most important variables. We shall focus mainly on Google, as it is the global search engine market leader. As illustrated in the table below, Google currently leads the search engine market with all others making up the remaining quarter of a percent.

Search Engine	Market Share
Google	76.51%
Yahoo!	12.64%
MSN	3.43%
Microsoft Live	2.6%
AOL	2.09%
ASK	1.53%
Others	1.2%

Table 1: Search Engine Market Share

These statistics were generated on Monday, December 31, 2007 at 2:47:03 AM, by www.hitslink.com.

As optimizing your Web site for a single search engine is dramatically easier and more cost effective than optimizing for multiple search engines, it makes sense to focus on activities which will produce the most results at the least cost. If you optimize your Web site for Google alone, you will draw more traffic than you could achieve by doing the same with all the other search engines put together.

Search Engine Optimization

However, we shall also cover information and techniques that will show you how to optimize for the other major search engines as well.

Chapter 2

Web Site Optimization

Getting Started

For a Web site to exist and be browsed to on the Internet, it needs to have a domain name and Internet protocol (IP) address. Without this they could not exist on the Internet, as the IP address is mapped to a domain name. This allows Web sites to be addressed by friendlier domain names such as (www.samuelblankson.com), rather than the less memorable and difficult to remember IP addresses (e.g., 83.170.64.93).

Normally Web sites on the World Wide Web are preceded by "www."; however, this is not strictlynecessary. Web sites can exist within domains as sub domains, or they can be private and obscured from the prying eyes of the general public. The space that a Web site occupies need not reside on a machine with the Web site's IP address. The Web site can be linked to storage elsewhere. In fact, a Web site can utilize many resources across the World Wide Web but seem like one coherent entity to the Web user.

What's In a Name

All SEO campaigns should begin with optimization of the Web site's pages; however, if you have not registered a domain name yet, you are in a unique position to get it right from the very start.

The domain name is the name you select for your Web site. It must be unique, as duplicates are not allowed on the Internet, therefore, if you are looking to register a new domain name, you may have to change your original preference or elect to have a domain name registered against another domain extension.

Domain Name Extension

Domain extensions end the domain address of a Web site. The .com extension is meant to represent U.S. commercial Web sites. It is so popular that Web site owners from around the world prefer it to any other extension, and so it does not always accurately represent the United States commercial Web sites anymore. The .org Web sites were meant to represent United States non-profit organization Web sites; however, this extension has also proven very popular and today is used by many Web sites who are far from being owned by U.S. non-profit organizations – such as www.practicalbooks.org.

There are many other domain extensions and almost every country is assigned one. There are also specialist domain extensions as well as reserved domain extensions used to administer the World Wide Web itself. Most Web users are used to .com and tend to assume that a site ends in .com unless told otherwise through marketing and promotion. If the .com extension is unavailable for your chosen domain name – as was the case for www.practicalbooks.com you may have to select .org, .net or any of the other extensions that are free to use with your chosen domain name, i.e., .tv, .biz, .co.uk, etc.

Domain Name

Another way around unavailable domain names is to slightly augment your chosen domain name in an attempt to create something new that is not already assigned. This option may also be chosen if your domain name is very commonly misspelled. For example, I could have tried the following options with my own Web site, as in these examples of commonly misspelled names:

www.practicalbooks.com
practicalbook.com
practicalbooks.org
practicallybooks.com
prakticalbooks.com
practikalbooks.com
practicalbooks.net

Table 2: Domain Name Alternatives

Unregistered Domain Names

If a domain name is parked and not being used as a Web site, you could check the expiration date of the registration, it may be coming up soon, in which case you could be lucky and the owner might relinquish control of the domain name, or otherwise fail to renew his/her registration. This frees the domain name and allows you to register it under your name.

Buying Domain Names

You could also try contacting the owner of the assigned Web site and asking them if they are prepared to sell you the domain name. This option is almost always more expensive and comes with some risks. Make sure you protect your interests and money by using an escrow lawyer or a solicitor, who will hold the payment between you and the domain name owner until the successful transfer of ownership can be confirmed. Try searching www.whois-search.com for the domain name details as proof of transfer of ownership. Once the transfer has been confirmed, the escrow lawyer can release the funds you deposited with the firm to the domain name seller.

Transfer Process

Transfer processes vary between domain name registrars. Visit www.nominet.org.uk for information on the transfer processes and fees for transferring .uk domain names. Similarly, visit www.networksolutions .com for most of the other domain names ending in .com, .biz, .bz, .cc, .gs, .info, .ms, .net, .org, .tc, .tv, .us, .vg and .ws, or visit www.icann.org for transfers between registrars.

Selecting a Domain Name

You can get your SEO off to a better start with a carefully selected domain name. While you can choose any name you want and market and promote it to success, it will be easier to choose already popular keyword(s) and start your advertising and awareness campaign a little further ahead. If you elect to do this, the name you select must be available, relevant and relate to your site's content and purpose.

A keyword tool that can help you find the most popular, yet least utilized relevant and topic related keywords to use in the selection of your Web site name is http://adwords.google.com/select/KeywordToolExternal.

Similarly, if you have not decided on the topic of your Web site, this tool can help you discover what is most popular on the World Wide Web. Selecting your domain name this way gives you a head start in the SEO battle. It also allows you to better focus your entire site towards maximizing its SEO.

Web Site

Not everyone can afford the luxury of choosing a SEO domain name and Web site topic. However, everyone can utilize the subject of the next section; optimizing the Web page's META data and the Web site content.

META Tags

META Tags: Optimizing Your Website for Internet Search Engines (ISBN: 190578998X), covers this subject in more detail; however, we will summarize the topics here.

Your entire Web page is represented by a coded language. This coded language is called Hyper Text Mark-up Language (HTML or XHTML, the latter being an extended version which requires tags to be properly closed). HTML uses tags to represent everything you see on a Web page. There are some main tags we will now examine in order to better understand META tags.

The first tag in most Web pages is the HTML tag. This tag is represented with <HTML> and has to be closed at the end of your Web page with </HTML>. The / represents an end to the tag name that follows it. In HTML, declared tags need to be closed with the / followed by the tag name.

You have to have HTML at the beginning of your Web site code, otherwise everything else you declare within the Web page code may appear as text in the browser page. After

HTML and before the BODY tag is the HEAD tag. Here is where the META tags and the TITLE tag are declared. These tell the browser and Web sites how to display and treat the Web page.

There are many META tags for making your Web site more index and catalog friendly, such as META tags that provide the creation date, author, copyright details, type of content (for censorship), application used to create the site, etc. In most cases, none of these META tags will assist search engines to place you at the top of their SERPs. Furthermore, because Google dominates the search engine market and does not heavily rely on META tags as did (and still do), some of the other search engines, it is not time well spent to pursue overuse of META tags. This is especially true for non-SEO driving META tags.

Therefore, we shall only focus on the handful of META tags which can be used to influence your Web site's SERPs position. These are namely the TITLE tag, the Description META tag, Revisit-After META tag, Refresh META tag, Robots META tag, and the Keywords META tag. For a full explanation of all of the META tags, you may reference the book, *META Tags: Optimizing Your Website for Internet Search Engines* (ISBN: 190578998X).

The TITLE Tag

The TITLE tag is not a META tag. However, TITLE can be declared either outside of the HEAD section or within the HEAD section. TITLE declares the title of the Web page. This title should be a concise distillation of the entire contents of the Web page. To get the most from the TITLE tag, first use a keyword tool such as the one provided by Google AdWords (http://adwords.google.com) to discover the most popular keywords relating to what the Web page covers. Create a title for your Web page out of the most relevant and popular keywords as possible. Focus on keywords that are popular, however not over subscribed for Google AdWords.

The different search engine's SERPs have different lengths that they limit TITLE tags to display. For instance,

Google and Microsoft Live limit titles to 65 characters (including spaces), and Yahoo! and AltaVista limit to 118 characters. To be on the safe side you should try to limit your Web page TITLE tags to 60 characters long. Your title will be cut off if it is too long.

To make it easier to cram in as many relevant keywords as possible to describe your site, you can use spaces, commas, other characters, e.g.: |, -, _, etc. Therefore, "Buy Office Furniture – Filing Cabinets, Chairs and Desks" or "Buy Office Furniture | Filing Cabinets | Chairs | Desks" are all acceptable. Limit the use of short words whenever possible, e.g.; it, as, of, in, by, my, I, for, your, etc. These words just take up space that could be used by a popular keyword. The syntax for the TITLE tag is in the following example:

<title>Title Text</title>

Therefore, if the title text is "Practical Books," the tag would read:

<title>Practical Books - Children | Fiction | Finance | Self Help | Music | Gambling</title>
N.B. "Practical Books - Children | Fiction | Finance | Self Help | Music | Gambling" in this case, is the title text.

The DESCRIPTION META Tag

The DESCRIPTION META tag is used to describe a Web page. Some search engines index this META tag and display it in their SERPs. It is crucial that your description contains all the major keywords relating to your Web page. Similarly, because the description will be displayed in the SERPs and thus read by Web users, it is also a good idea for it to be readable, interesting and informative, rather than a list of keywords only.

There is some ambiguity as to whether Google uses this META tag in resolving ranking. However, Google advises that a unique DESCRIPTION META tag be used for each page, rather than the same description for each page on your site.

Search Engine Optimization

Where Google and Lycos are purposely secretive and vague, other search engines are more clear about the importance of the DESCRIPTION META tag in resolving ranking. Table 3 illustrates the treatment and importance of META tags and the TITLE tag in helping resolve ranking at some of the top search engines.

Search Engine	TITLE Tag	META Tags
AltaVista	Very important, should be unique for every page.	Not important, but should be included just in case.
DMOZ Users: AOL, Netscape; AltaVista, HotBot, Google and Lycos directories.	No, but advised.	No, but the description and keywords usage is advised.
Google	Not known, but seems to be a factor.	No, but unique description is advised.
HotBot	Very important.	Very important, both description (150 characters) and keywords (75 characters).
Lycos	Not known, but seems to be a factor.	Not mentioned.
MSN and Live	Important, include keywords.	Both are supported; description limited to 250, keywords to 1017.
Yahoo! Directory	No, but advised. Make concise.	No, but the description and keywords usage are advised.

Table 3: Search Engine Usage of META and TITLE tags

The syntax for the DESCRIPTION META Tag:

<meta name="description" content="Description text">

or

<meta content="Description text" name="description" >

As an example, the DESCRIPTION META tag for practicalbooks.org could look like this:

<meta content="Official home of books by Samuel Blankson. Download free previews and review each book before you buy. Find a book on tax, sci-fi, gambling, self help, SEO and more." name="description">

It is difficult to say how much the DESCRIPTION META tag plays in the resolving page ranking on SERPs. However, as the DESCRIPTION META tag is displayed on SERPs, it makes good sense to include it. Include a different and relevant DESCRIPTION META tag per page whenever you can. Keywords within the description are only important if they will help entice readers to visit your Web page. The most important aspect of the DESCRIPTION META tag is that it must correctly describe your Web page, and describe it in such a way as to entice, seduce, encourage and "force" readers to want to find out more by visiting your Web page.

> **WARNING**: The KEYWORD META tags should be used with some caution, as abuse can cause your site to be black-listed or dropped in ranking by search engines. Make sure that the keywords you use are all supported by keywords in your TITLE tag or on your Web page.

The KEYWORDS META Tag

The KEYWORD META tag is used by search engines to properly index your site. It is especially useful for adding synonyms to the support keywords already on your Web page. You can also add key phrases and search terms to the list of keywords. Keywords are perhaps best separated with a comma, e.g., "book, book of the year, bestselling books, SEO books," and so on.
The KEYWORD META tag syntax:

<META NAME="keywords" CONTENT="list of comma separated keywords">

Or

```
<META CONTENT="list of comma separated keywords",
NAME="keywords" >
```

An example of keywords for a calendar Web site could be:

```
<meta content="calendar, calendars, calender, calandar,
calendar"NAME="keywords">
```

Other META Tags

There are many other META tags; however, the most useful for SEO are the DESCRIPTION and KEYWORD META tags previously discussed. The majority of the other META tags are harmless and generally ignored by search engines, especially for determining page rank. Some META tags such as the AUTHOR META tag and the COPYRIGHT META tag are useful for providing information about the Web page or Web document. These META tags are harmless to you and to search engine's ranking algorithms. They are thus useless for improving your Web page ranking on SERPs. They are useful pieces of information to include and can generally be added, removed or amended centrally for every page in your Web site using most Web authoring tools such as Microsoft FrontPage, or DreamWeaver.

Other META tags such as the REFRESH, ROBOTS and REVISIT-AFTER META tags, although ignored by most of the major search engines, can cause your Web site harm if you over abuse their usage. This is especially true of the REFRESH META tag. The META tag allows you to set a delay and a forwarding page from any page in your Web site. This META tag can be abused by redirecting visitors from a high ranking Web page to a lower ranking page. Its use is generally frowned upon and considered as spam sites. This can get you black-listed, especially if visitors complain. Furthermore, some search engines can detect this usage and will either penalize your ranking or black-list your Web site.

The ROBOTS META Tag

The ROBOTS META tag can be used to control which pages of your Web site the search engine robots can index and follow links from. This META tag is really meant for users who cannot upload and control the /robots.txt file on their Web server. Good robots will obey this META tag; however, bad robots mining for data will completely ignore this META tag. If you have control of the /robots.txt file for your Web site, it is advisable that you use it to control robots following all your Web links and indexing all your Web pages.

Robots.txt File

The robots.txt file is simply that—a file called robots.txt which is stored in the root directory of your Web site. This file should contain the following text:

User-agent: *
Disallow:

The asterisk after User-agent: indicates that the following restriction is to apply to all robots visiting the site. A robots name could be used instead of User-agent: *, i.e., User-agent: Googlebot. *See* jafsoft/searchengines/webbots.html for a list of robot names. The Disallow: line should list all directories to which the named robot(s) is to be restricted access. Please note you cannot restrict access to a file or group of files. You can only restrict access to a directory, therefore you may need to move all your restricted files to a private folder and restrict that folder. The / (forward slash) symbol denotes a restriction; therefore to exclude all robots from the server you would use the following:

User-agent: *
Disallow: /

While to exclude all robots from parts of a server, you would use:

User-agent: *
Disallow: /private/
Disallow: /pwd/
Disallow: /scripts/

To exclude a single robot from the server (e.g., Googlebot):

User-agent: Googlebot

Disallow: /

And to exclude a single robot from parts of a server (i.e., AltaVista-Intranet), you would use the following:

User-agent: AltaVista-Intranet
Disallow: /private/
Disallow: /pwd/
Disallow: /scripts/

> **WARNING:** Use the robots.txt option with caution. You could block all your efforts at SEO if you accidentally restrict robots access to index your Web site.

The REVISIT-AFTER META Tag

You can tell robots when to revisit your Web site. This seems useful, especially if your site changes frequently and you wish to assist the search engine indexing process to keep up to date with your site's changes. I say this seems useful because it is actually no longer very useful. This is especially true of the large search engines. These search engines schedule their own revisit cycle and will ignore the REVISIT-AFTER META tag. It is almost a waste of time to maintain this META tag. Similarly, those who attempt to abuse this META tag, in an attempt to raise their page rankings on SERPs can be punished with a demotion of their page rank. Long gone are the days when you can set the REVISIT-AFTER META tag and fool robots to revisit your site daily in a hope to improve your Web page ranking.

> **WARNING**: If you set the frequency of the revisits to a high number such as once daily and your site content does not change frequently enough to justify this, some search engines could penalize you for this abuse. Googlebot ignores this META tag, however some smaller search engine robots do not.

Sitemaps

A sitemap is a listing of all URLs for a Web site. This includes Web pages and other files (e.g., PDF, .TXT or .DOC files, etc.) on your Web site. A sitemap file should be written or generated in XML format. Within this file (normally sitemap.xml) should be listed: your Web page, file URLs, last modified dates, frequency of change and priority relative to other pages on the site.

Sitemaps allow search engines to more intelligently crawl your Web site. They also allow you to control how search engines prioritize your Web pages. Additionally, they allow you to specify the frequency of change your pages undergo; allowing search engine robots to better manage revisits.

Google, Yahoo! and Microsoft, as well as many other search engines, all support Sitemaps. The format for your site map should be as follows:

```
<?xml version="1.0" encoding="utf-8"?>
<urlset xmlns="http://www.sitemapsorg/schemas/sitemap/0.9"
>
    <url>
      <loc>http://www.practicalbooks.org/</loc>
  <priority>1.0</priority>
  <lastmod>2008-03-14T02:58:12-05:00</lastmod>
  <changefreq>monthly</changefreq>
    </url>
    <url>
      .
      .
      .
    </url>
</urlset>
```

Note that each Web page or Web document should be specified within the <url> and </url> tags. You must specify <loc> and </loc> for each url listed; however, <lastmod>, </lastmod>, <changefreq>, </changefreq>, <priority> and </priority> are optional tags.

Visit www.sitemaps.org/protocol.php for more details on the Sitemaps XML format. Normally if you have over 10,000 URLs it is advised to use multiple sitemaps.

Writing sitemaps can be very time consuming; therefore, you may wish to use a script to automatically generate your sitemap. Visit http://sitemap .xmlecho.org/sitemap/ or search for "sitemap generator" on Google for a list of free or low cost sitemap generators. Some sitemap generators are scripts that may require specific scripting language support, such as Python. Search http://sourceforge.net/ for "sitemap generator" for a list of these tools.

Once you have generated a sitemap, you need to place the file on your Web server preferably in the root directory. Next, you either need to submit the sitemap to Google, Yahoo! and the other search engines, or simply wait until their crawler next visits your Web site. The following are links for submitting your Sitemap to the major search engines:

- http://search.msn.com/docs/submit.aspx
- https://siteexplorer.search.yahoo.com/submit
- https://www.google.com/webmasters/tools

Google specifically accepts sitemap submissions while the others pick up the sitemap file when their robot next crawls your Web site.

Maximizing Your Sitemap

Sitemaps are great to use as an SEO tool for your Web site. To maximize your Sitemap for SEO, you will need to create many keyword dense Web pages, or write articles laden with specific and relevant keywords that support your Web site content. Within these articles, or promotional Web pages, include links to the relevant pages within your Web site. Next, include the URLs to these articles or pages in your XML sitemap file and set the priorities for these pages high (as close to 1.00 as you want). Finally, submit your sitemap to Google, Yahoo! and MSN Live.

Web Site Content

After optimizing the TITLE tags and META tags for your pages, you can turn to the page content; this is the actual substance of your Web page. Here is where it pays to know how to write compelling text that is interesting, relevant, purposeful, informative and unique – wherever possible.

Before we delve deep into this topic, let us consider an obvious yet often overlooked point. What text is most relevant to your Web site? You may say, "Well, all of it surely?" WRONG. Search engines tend to focus more on the top section of your Web pages rather than the bottom section. Therefore, it is vital that all your top keywords are represented in the top section of your HTML code (or Web page).

WARNING: Google's Web Master Guidelines specifically speak against certain SEO practices. The following is a brief list of practices to avoid.

The Google Warning

In this section we will cover many topics that are frowned upon by search engines. Please read the Google Web Master Guidelines carefully before reading any further.

- Avoid hidden text or hidden links.
- Don't use cloaking or sneaky redirects.
- Don't send automated queries to Google.
- Don't load pages with irrelevant keywords.
- Don't create multiple pages, subdomains or domains with substantially duplicate content.
- Don't create pages that install viruses, trojans or other badware.
- Avoid "doorway" pages created just for search engines or other "cookie cutter" approaches such as affiliate programs, with little or no original content.

- If your site participates in an affiliate program, make sure that your site adds value. Provide unique and relevant content that gives users a reason to visit your site first.

Read Google's complete list at the following Web page: www.google.com/support/webmasters/bin/answer.py?answer= 35769

Optimizing for Search Engine Relevance

We have briefly looked at META tag optimization, now let's turn our attention to keyword and query, or search term optimization. The main purpose of keyword and search term optimization is to increase the perceived relevance of a Web page. I say perceived because of how a search engine views the relevance of a Web page, and the actual relevancy are not always identical.

Some Web pages are full of irrelevant nonsense; a search will find them at the top of the SERPs. This is because these clever Web masters have made their Web site look extremely relevant to the search engine. You can also elevate your Web page's relevance to certain keywords and search terms by using various term boosting techniques.

Term Boosting

To apply term boosting, first identify the most popular search terms you wish to be associated with your Web site. A few years ago, I undertook an experiment to test the power of term boosting. I chose the search term "Samuel Blankson", a virtually unknown search term before 2001. Today a search for "Samuel Blankson" on Google returns over 82,300 results, Yahoo! returns 98,200, and MSN returns 23,200. This is the power of SEO and term boosting.

Term boosting can be applied to your Web page address (URL), the text attached to links to your Web page, your Web page content (especially the section closest to the top of the page), your META KEYWORD and META DESCRIPTION tags. We have already covered META tags, but it is worth mentioning that you can and should use key phrases wherever possible, in place of single keywords, unless the keywords are very rare and hardly used on the Internet.

You should avoid pronouns, auxiliary verbs, conjunctions, grammatical articles or articles, as these are a waste of opportunities to repeat keywords and keyword phrases. Because keywords are targeted by everyone on the World Wide Web, you stand a better chance of gaining relevance for your page by using key phrases. "Best search engine optimization book" or "best search engine optimization books" is a better boost than simply, "book" or "books".

We have already discussed how you can use keywords in your domain name. You can also extend this to your Web page URL names within your Web site. Calling a page "nonfiction_books.htm" is more useful than "nfb1.htm". Similarly, calling an image "image1.gif", serves you less than calling it "science_fiction_book.gif". You cannot use spaces in URLs, therefore you have to substitute spaces with underscores or dashes.

You can attach text to the links you specify on your Web page from other pages. You should do this whether these links are on your Web site or are from other Web sites. The syntax is as follows:

<a href="the link address"> the text </a>

as an example;

<a href="www.samuelblankson.com"> The official home of Samuel Blankson - biography, Samuel Blankson books, calendars, Ultimate Roulette System gambling strategy, Ultimate gambling systems casino, Uju music </a>

Make your text relevant, specific and include appropriate keywords in your search terms wherever possible.

Each link, image and object should be correctly tagged with keywords and key phrases. The aim here is to increase the key phrase and keyword density of your Web page. The more key phrases are repeated on your Web site, while maintaining sense and user friendly readability of the Web page, the better.

In-page bookmark links can be employed to link to sections within the same page. The link text associated with these can be used to boost key phrases and keywords. The syntax is as follows:

```
<a name="text to appear on webpage" title="link text."
href="#bookmark link.">
```

Here is an example of its usage:

```
<a name="Samuel_Blankson" title="Author of Samuel
Blankson books, creator of the Ultimate Roulette System
gambling strategy software, and songwriter."
href="#About_the_author">
```

You must first create the bookmarks before you can link to them. Search with the help files associated with your Web authoring software to discover how you can use it to create bookmarks.

WARNING: Avoid gibberish and nonsensical Web content and link text, as this does more harm to your page ranking and SEO strategy than good. It could also cause search engines to lower your ranking.

Link Boosting

We shall now look at how you can improve your ranking through your links. Page ranking is calculated based on several principles; one of these is link popularity. This is determined by how many Web pages are linked to your Web page (inbound links) and what their page rank is. Another criteria is how many sites you are linking to, (outbound links) and where their page rank currently stands.

The amount of outbound links on a page determines how easy it is for a visitor to leave that page and this lowers your page rank; therefore, it is prudent to limit the number of exiting links from your Web pages. It is also prudent to have links to other pages in your Web site; however, avoid unending loops (also called sinks). These are links to pages which link back in a closed loop to the originating page, with no exit links out of the loop. Sinks are penalized with lower page ranks by search engines.

If you must have links to the outside, try to group them onto a single page such as a "links" page. This serves to do several things. It aids your purpose of having the links and it dilutes the usefulness of the back-links from your site. This is because many outbound links on a page mean the probability of anyone of them being used to exit your site reduces dramatically, therefore the rank gain they would get from the link is minimized. The links page rank will suffer greatly, but the rest of your Web site pages will not.

The ranking system assumes that the more pages a Web site has, the higher a rank it deserves; because there will be more information there than at smaller sites matching the same search terms. It is therefore wise to spread your content across as many pages as is sensible to do. Some Web masters have taken this to the extreme by displaying only one paragraph per page, thus creating a Web site with thousands of pages just to cover a topic that would otherwise fit on a Web site with a few hundred, longer pages.

Page rank is greatly improved by inbound links from high page-ranked sites to your Web pages. You can create these back-links manually or in many cases automatically with a robot or a computer program. The following is a list of methods and sources for improving your page ranking through links to your Web pages or Web site:

1. Web sites with guest books.
2. Forums.
3. Discussion groups.
4. Wikis (some use <rel= "nofollow">), which tells search engines to allow links into Wikis to count towards the Wiki site's page rank, but not the other way around, therefore linking to them has little to no positive effect on your page rank.
5. Sites which facilitate reviewing of products and allow Web links within the review.

6. Press releases and articles with your Web link in the signature, or within the article.

7. e-Zines and newsletter ads. Create a newsletter and submit this to your customer base via e-mail. You can also submit details of the e-zines to search engine directories with a link to your site.

8. Negotiate links from related sites. This involves contacting your competitors or Web sites that are hosting related content to your site, and asking them to include your Web site link on their site; preferably for free. Normally they will want to exchange links with you or charge you a fee. This method can be extremely time-consuming and frustrating, especially when they have a higher page rank than you. Their terms can often seem unreasonable.

9. It is wise to seek high ranking, free sources for back-linking first, before venturing to the costlier methods of press releases, link exchanges and reciprocal back-linking. Many free press release sites exist today. To access these, simply search for "free press release" on any search engine. They are free and easy to use, you simply do one of the following:

    a. Sign the guest books with your Web site address in the signature.
    b. Post a comment in the forum again with your Web site address as the signature.
    c. Post an article or review with your Web site address in the signature.

The only downside to this is that it is time consuming when properly done. You can also use a robot or small program or script to automatically search the World Wide Web for forums, Wikis and discussion groups to post your Web site link.

Link Farming

You can also employ a link farm to boost your Web site's page ranking. This is a lot more costly and even more time consuming. To do this, you need to set up a link community; which is a group of Web sites that have several high ranking sites linking to them and they in turn link to each other.

Once these sites are well ranked by search engines you then have every page on them linking to your new Web site. This will raise your new Web site's ranking immediately. If you cannot afford the money or time to employ this technique, do not worry. Many people on the Web offer this service for a fee. Look on any search engine for "improve your page rank" and you will find these services.

> **WARNING:** Be cautious about page rank boosting service providers. Most will not help your ranking. Instead, they will likely post your Web link at low to unranked pages across the Internet. Even if they do deliver the 60,000+ back-links as promised, you may find your site's rank does not budge. Seek quality (and costlier) service providers, or simply bite the bullet, and do it yourself.

Link Authority

A link authority is useful to employ if you cannot afford to build and maintain a link farm. You can set up a link authority, which is a site that has a large amount of outgoing links to highly ranked Web sites such as the following:

- www.facebook.com
- www.google.com
- www.hi5.com
- www.live.com
- www.msn.com
- www.myspace.com
- www.orkut.com
- www.wikipedia.org

- www.yahoo.com
- www.youtube.com

It also helps to have a couple of highly ranked sites back-linking to the link authority. Make sure your link authority follows the rules already discussed, i.e., has many informative pages, does not have too many outgoing links per page, etc. Once the link authority becomes highly ranked, you can add links from every page possible to your low ranked Web site, instantly improving the new sites ranking.

Content Hiding

Once you create the perfect content and upload it online, it is very easy for your competitors to view your HTML code, see why you are being rated so high and simply copy you. To avoid this and also to hide your term boosting from the eyes of the general Web site visitor, you could consider hiding your content. There are several options available to you; these are text hiding, link hiding, META refresh, and encryption.

WARNING: Search engine directories which are maintained by humans, rather than automatic software, frown on this type of SEO, and you could be banned from registering on them or your ranking reduced severely if your Web site employs this technique. The search engines that use robots to crawl through Web sites tend to be less sensitive to text and link hiding, however even these crawlers use human Web site auditors who randomly select sites to check. Again, be aware you could be penalized for using these techniques; however, some believe the benefits are worth the risks.

Text Hiding

Term boosting can make your pages look unsightly and deter visitors if taken to the extreme. This is because you may have multiple repetitions of search terms and keywords, making the content almost unreadable. To get around this problem, you can hide the text using the background color of the Web page. You can also dramatically reduce the font size of the term boosting text. This may fool some search engines and thus allow your site to gain rank. Remember also that the top section of your Web page is where content is most effectively placed.

Link Hiding

Having many outbound links from a page may look suspicious to visitors, and can detract from the effectiveness of your Web site; therefore you may want to hide them from your visitors. To do this you can assign each link to a single pixel of your background image. You can even place this single pixel at the top of your Web site without detracting from your Web site's look, feel and visitor friendliness.

The syntax for this is:

< a href="the weblink/">< img src= "location of single pixel file">< /a>

As an example:

< a href="samuelblankson/">< img src="samuelblankson/images/onepixel.gif">< /a>

You have to first create a single pixel image and color it the same color as the background of your Web site. Once this is done, you simply place the image on your Web page and assign the link as you would do to any image.

META REFRESH Tag

Using a heavily keyworded phrase or link boosted page will help your SEO at search engine SERPs. However, as soon as anyone visits your site they will most likely leave because the content will be unreadable. To get around this you can use a doorway page. Doorway pages are more geared towards fooling search engine robots. The robots fetch the home page of a site and proceed to crawl through all the links on that page. Therefore, if you could present a heavily search-term boosted page to these robots, while presenting a totally different -- more visitor friendly -- page to human visitors, you could achieve both objectives at the same time.

This is possible through several means. The first and simplest is to use the META REFRESH tag. By setting the duration between presenting the doorway page and jumping to the next page to zero, you allow robots to download and capture the doorway page, however, to the human visitor it will seem as if your Web site homepage page is the redirected page. This is because the transition between the doorway and redirected pages happened too fast for human comprehension.

The META REFRESH tag is a HTTP header used by the Web server that the Web page resides on. What this means is that it instructs the Web browser to redirect or reload the Web page. It is a useful tool for reloading a page when you have dynamically changing data which you would like constantly refreshed or it can also be used to redirect a Web page to another Web page. This is the use we will focus on.
The syntax for this is as follows:

```
<meta http-equiv="refresh" content="duration in
seconds;url=full website address to redirect to">
```

As an example to redirect a Web browser to jump to www. practicalbooks.org immediate upon arriving at a site, you would use:

```
<meta http-equiv="refresh"
content="0;url=practicalbooks.org">
```

This technique is also termed *cloaking*.

WARNING: Although you may be using a duration of zero seconds, the Web browser could still take a few seconds to redirect, so make sure whatever the visitor sees on the first page is presentable and professional. On older Web browsers visitors will not be able to go back after the redirect. Make sure you put the right address in for the redirection; as a redirection to a non-existent page will cause you to lose that visitor permanently. Most of the top ten search engines' robots are aware of this technique and will dump the doorway page, replacing it with the redirected page. You stand a better chance of fooling robots with a script of some kind.

You can achieve the same results that the META REFRESH tag does using scripts. A script is a small software code that performs a function. A quick search on Google for "page redirect script" should yield some examples of ready written scripts to do exactly that. There are some limitations with scripts, such as lack of support on older Web browsers or security restrictions on the host machine. Keep this in mind when deciding whether to go with a META REFRESH tag or a script.

Encryption

If you are going to use a doorway page as described in the last discussion section, then you might want to go one step further and encrypt your Web site entirely. Encryption allows you to totally hide your page's HTML from all others. Unfortunately, this would include search engine robots. However, if you use a doorway page which forwards visitors to your encrypted page, you will avoid the vast majority of the negatives of encryption and SEO. Encryption allows you to hide the code of your Web pages from your competitors, plagiarists and hackers. If you have something valuable to hide within the code of your site then this is definitely an option you should consider. Again, a quick search on Google for "Web page encryption" will yield many sources and software that will assist you in doing this.

Search Engine Submissions

Search engines that employ crawlers, eventually get to all new Web sites and index them; however, if you cannot wait the (possible) months it could take, then you can submit your site to the search engines directly. Doing this allows you to have your site indexed within a matter of days rather than months. The days where you could submit to search engines for free are quickly disappearing. In today's atmosphere, you should expect to part with some money for the service. Only a few search engines still accept free submissions, however almost all the *directories* do accept free submissions. A few search engines have now gone 100% pay-per-click and you cannot submit your site to them even if you wanted to. You can however, submit a pay-per-click advertisement with them. We shall look at pay-per-click, in the upcoming chapter.

You can submit your Web site address, topic and your contact details to the major search engines manually or automatically via a submission agent. For the small fees involved, it is probably not worth your time to submit manually. There are service providers on the World Wide Web, who specialize in search engine submission, however a word of caution, don't be fooled by the providers who claim to be able to submit your site to 10,000 search engines.

One reason is that the 10 largest search engines service over 99% of the global search engine market; therefore, why bother submitting to 10,000? Or even 1,000? There are also "Free-For-All" (FFA) sites that allow anyone to list their Web site on their directories. These sites make up the majority of the 10,000 search engines that the search engine submission service providers (offering huge submissions results) use. Submitting to these FFA sites does nothing great for your page rank or popularity. This is because they are mostly zero page-ranked, and so heavily utilized that in some cases your link would last less than a few days on their pages before newer submissions force yours off the list.

Furthermore, getting listed on certain FFA's could actually harm your page ranking. This is because anyone can list on them, allowing nefarious people carrying out illegal and often immoral activities via their Web site flock to them. Avoid these large submission offers like the plague.

Stick with the top 10 search engines. You can buy a submission service to automatically submit to as many of the top search engines as possible. Where they stop, you can continue to either submit manually to the remainder of the search engines, or simply wait until their crawler visits your Web site. The top ten search engines and directories are Google, Yahoo!, MSN Live, AOL, Ask, AltaVista, FAST, GigaBlast, Snap and LookSmart. The following submission addresses cover all the free submission search engines and directories in the top ten list (please note that some of these links supply data to more than one directory:

- http://search.msn.com.sg/docs/submit.aspx
- https://siteexplorer.search.yahoo.com/submit
- https://siteexplorer.searchyahoo/submit
- www.gigablast.com/addurl
- www.google.co.uk/addurl

This is a listing of all the English speaking US centric search engines. The majority of these search engines offer search services in most of the major languages around the world, as well as offering localized and regional search services across the globe. In the next section there are more details concerning foreign search engines. *See also,* Foreign Search Engine Listing; Appendix 2.

Directory Manual Submissions

Search engines are not the only major source of information on the Internet. Internet directories are another large contender. In fact, nowadays almost every search engine either subscribes to or maintains its own directory. These directories normally are populated by Web site owners who seek to be listed in the directories so that they can get more traffic and thus improve their page rank.

Most, if not all of these directories are manually maintained. Submissions are vetted by humans and thus they tend to contain cleaner data than the search engine indexes do. However, because these directories are a list of the sites whose owners have bothered to get listed, they can sometimes seem to be incomprehensive. They are the yellow pages of the Internet. If you don't submit your Web site and get it accepted, it simply will not be featured there.

Although the majority of these directories are free to submit to, a few of them are not. This is normally a one time fee or an annual renewal fee. This trend is likely to continue as more and more directories seek to become profitable, rather than dependent on the generosity of their search engine based owners. There are manual directory submission service providers available on the World Wide Web; however, their services are not free. Also, they can often make mistakes in the category in which they register your site on.

More important than manually submitting to search engines is manually submitting to directories. Directories are categorized into distinct general categories. When you submit to them, you need to identify which category or subcategory best describes your Web site content. A mistake made here, could sentence your site to a life of obscurity on that directory. Clearly identify which category your Web site belongs to before submitting it. You will have to specify this category or subcategory during the submission process. Unlike the majority of search engine submissions, with directory submissions there are no guarantees that your Web site will be accepted by the person who makes the decision. The following is a list of popular directories across various regions:

POPULAR DIRECTORIES	
Best of the Web: Cost of this service is an annually recurring review fee of $79.95; or a one-time fee of $239.95.	Submit to: http://botw.org/helpcenter /submitcommercial.aspx
GoGuides: All Easy Submissions require a one-time review fee of $69.95 USD.	Submit to: goguides.org/info/addurl.htm
Google Directory: Powered by the Open Directory Project (OPD).	Submit: Use the Open Directory Project (See below).
JoeAnt: Volunteer built directory.	Submit to: joeant/suggest.html
Open Directory Project: DMOZ	Submit to: dmoz.org/add.html
Skaffe International Directory: Human edited international directory filtered for spam and adult content.	Submit to: skaffe/info/addurl.php
WebSavvy Directory: Single Review PinCodes are available for $33.00 via PayPal at www.paypal.com. Single Review PinCodes may be used one time only. Sites will be reviewed within 48 hours or less. Multiple Review PinCodes are available for $300.00 per year.	Submit to: websavvy.cc/add.php
Yahoo! Directory: Paid submission review $299.00 USD (Renewed annually).	Submit to: https://ecom.yahoo/dir/express /intro
Gimpsy: Active Sites for Active People. Cost of the Promotion Option is just $40.00 USD! If your site is not approved, you will be refunded $20.00. New! Free use of Strongest Links for 180 days! (Worth $90.00).	Submit to: gimpsy/gimpsy/searcher /suggest.php

Table 4: Popular Directories

Building Back-Links

We have already covered how you can manually, or by using a script or robot, build back-links at forums, guestbooks, review sites, etc. We also touched briefly on the manual method of contacting Web owners and asking them to display your Web link in their sites; either through a one way, reciprocal or paid arrangement. In the next section we shall investigate this in detail.

Perhaps the best way to build quality back-links to your Web site is through someone linking to you. This could happen because your site provides useful, quality content or bad quality content, or a design causing people to link to you to show how *not* to do things. Whatever the reason you get back-linked, be thankful, traffic is traffic and page rank increase is what we all seek to achieve using SEO.

If you waited for people to link to you out of interest, pity or luck, you could be in for a very long wait. This leaves only one option, you have to do *something* to get people linking to your Web pages.

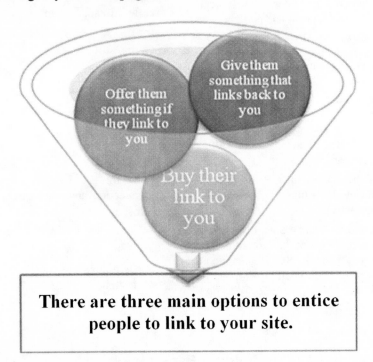

There are three main options to entice people to link to your site.

Let us look at the first option, "Give them something that links back to you". Many people use this option on the Internet. You may have seen the BBC news streamer that has a link back to BBC.co.uk. Every time someone embeds it into their Web site, they are in effect creating a back-link to the

BBC Web. Similarly, Amazon, Google toolbar and many other small applets or useful devices can be imbedded into your site. This gives added service and functionality to your visitors, which may actually be linking to a third-party.

You can do this as easily as anyone else. Simply by creating an applet and promoting it to Web masters as a tool or a gadget, that will somehow improve their Web site. Make sure your Web site link is imbedded in the applet and cannot be removed. It is not only toolbars and applets that can be used, but affiliations, newsletters, articles and press releases, are all other ways this can be achieved.

In the case of affiliation, not only do you offer Web masters a useful tool/product or feature to add to their site, but they can actually make a commission on every sale made through your link.

In the case of newsletters, articles or press releases, you can assign your Web link as part of the signature of the text. Web sites that feature your news release, article or newsletter will help to promote your page rank. Note that some sites strip out links on the articles and press releases that they feature, so placing the link within the release is a good idea.

Using Link Exchanges

Contacting individual Web sites to negotiate link placements and link exchanges can be time consuming and frustrating. You can get through more numbers of Web sites using a link exchange service. Simply search for "link exchange" on any search engine and you will be presented with a broad choice of providers. Link exchange providers come in two main groups: free and fee based.

Free link exchange service providers mainly require that you place their applet—which will display other people's links—on your Web site in exchange for your link to be displayed on other's Web sites. The principle is simple; for their time and effort they get free promotion of their service, and the improvement of their page rank, which they often use to sell other products, such as page rank boosting services.

The service normally works on a 2 to 1 or similar display ratio. This means every two links displayed on their applet at your site, they promise to display your link once, on an applet somewhere else.

The charging services offer the same features most of the time, however they refine their client list; categorize and try to keep your link displayed on relevant sites. Other charging link exchanges act as high page rank link brokers. They will typically have a list of high page ranked sites on their "books". These will be priced depending on the page rank of your Web link display duration (i.e., by week, month, year, etc.).

WARNING: Link Exchanges often have well written disclaimer documents, freeing them from the consequence of changing page rank after you purchase the service. Therefore, you may buy a PR8 service only to discover afterwards that the site is no longer a PR8, but has slipped to PR6. Another trick to be aware of is the advertisement of a page rank for the home page. After you buy the service you discover that your link has been placed on a lower ranked sub page on the Web site. Make sure you inquire into exactly where your link will be placed, and confirm the current page rank of that page before paying for the service.

Referrals

One of the best ways to promote your Web site or Web page, is to let others (yes, complete strangers), promote it for you. If you offer something unique, useful, exemplary, humorous, strange or in any way extraordinary, people will talk and share it with friends, colleagues and family. To facilitate this, always provide a share this link/site/article /product/review with a friend button. This allows visitors who have enjoyed, benefited or liked what you offer to e-mail the link to their friends. Depending on what you are offering, referral promotion will either work for you online, offline or both.

To set yourself up to benefit from this type of promotion, first make sure you offer a service that is second to none. A great product also goes a long way. Then, make sure you offer visitors an easy means of referring your site either through a, "Tell a friend..." link or via a testimonial-capturing feature on your site. A simple, "Did you enjoy our service? Tell others about it..." or similar option on your Web site can be used to capture testimonials.

Foreign Language Search Engines

It is not just English speaking people who use the Internet. All language speakers have access to the same services that you may enjoy over the Web. They are also looking for information, services and products. To reach these Internet users requires submitting to the search engines they use. However, because the language is different and regional preferences and cultural differences vary greatly, the way you promote should and will, have to change in these markets.

Apart from submitting your site to the non-English language search engines (see the listing below for some of these), you will also need to consider how you will deal with the language and cultural differences. In the next section we look at solutions to this problem.

FOREIGN LANGUAGE SEARCH ENGINES

Canada

Bellzinc.ca- Submit to:	directory.bellzinc.ca/bellzinc/english/queries/c_reg.asp
Canada One Business Directory - Submit to:	canadaone/business/addurl.html
CANLinks - Submit to:	canlinks.net/addalink

China

Baidu	http://site.baidu.com
Yasou	http://site.yahoo.com.cn
Sogou	www.sogou.com/dir
Sina	http://dir.iask.com
Netease	http://dir.so.163.com
Zhongsou	www.zhongsou.com
Google China	www.google.com/dirhp?hl=zh-CN&tab=wd&q=
Myrice	http://search.myrice.com/dir.htm
Tom	http://search.tom.com/dir

Germany

Allesklar	Listings starting at 199,00 EUR (Annual Renewal) - Submit: allesklar.de/listing.php, Free Submit: https://listing.allesklar.de/mt_shop/mt_basisdesc.php
Bellnet	Free listing or express listing (50 EUR) - Submit: bellnet.de/suchen/anmeldungsseite.html
ODP- Submit to:	dmoz.de/World/Deutsch
Sharelook Deutschland	Free listing or express listing (98 EUR) - Submit: sharelook.de
WEB.DE	Listings start at 180 EUR (Annual Renewal) - Submit: eintragsservice.web.de

FOREIGN LANGUAGE SEARCH ENGINES	
Submit German:	www.dmoz.org/World/Deutsch/Regi onal/Europa/Schweiz

Switzerland

AllesKlar (Germany)	Free listing or express listings starting at 199,00 EUR (Annual Renewal) - Search: allesklar.ch/ - Submit: https://listing.allesklar.de/mt_portal. php
Manitoo	Free listings or express listing (50,00 CHF) - Search: manitoo.ch/ - Free Submit: www.manitoo.ch/promotion/inscript ion_gratuite.php
Express Submit to:	manitoo.ch/promotion/inscription_e xpresse.php
ODP -Search:	dmoz.org
Yahoo! (Germany) - Free listing in Yahoo!'s European directories (except UK)	www.de.yahoo
Yoodle- Search:	www.yoodle.ch

Israel

Walla—Submit to:	buy.walla.co.il/ts.cgi?tsscript=guide/ add.site
Tapuz—Submit to:	tapuz.co.il/index/add.asp
Nana—Submit to:	index.nana.co.il/addsite/addsite.asp
Science—Submit to:	science.co.il/contact.asp
Open Directory Project Hebrew—Submit to:	dmoz.org.il
Open Directory Project Israel— Submit to:	dmoz.org/Regional/Middle_East/Israel

Italy

Submit Italian:	www.dmoz.org/World/Italiano/Regi

FOREIGN LANGUAGE SEARCH ENGINES	
	onale/Europa/Svizzera/
Sharelook.ch - Free listing or express listing (98,00 EUR) - Search: Choose an appropriate category and click on Neueintrag (left side).	www.sharelook.ch
France	
Submit French:	dmoz.org/World/Français/Régional/ Europe/Suisse

Table 5: Foreign Language Search Engines

Internet users from around the globe use three top-level, major search engines; with Google leading them all. The top search engines: Google, Yahoo!, MSN (which is powered by Windows Live), and AOL (which is powered by Google), all provide foreign language specific searching. Find them at the following links:

1. http://world.yahoo.com
2. www.google.com/language_tools?hl=en (scroll to the end for a full listing)
3. www.msn.com/worldwide.aspx

Foreign Language Web Site Translation

The search engines also offer language translation features and services, however be warned that what comes out of the translator may not be what you want your visitor to read. If anything, using an online, real-time translator of your Web pages may drive traffic back out of your site. Therefore, some professional translation, keywords and content optimization of your site is required.

There are several ways to tackle this problem one of which is that you can use multilingual SEO techniques to create language specific doorway pages. These will in turn help drive traffic to your English site through a language specific doorway page. This solution assumes and depends on the fact that most Internet users can speak or understand some level of English; therefore it draws them to your site in their native language.

Moving on from the doorway page, they will have to switch to English. This is a useful technique for sites that offer products and services not specific to a particular region or language; however, sites that offer information only, fall short of being useful when this technique is applied to them. You can find multilingual SEO service providers by searching for "multilingual SEO" via any search engine.

The technique is useful for attracting foreign visitors who may understand English. Unlike most English speakers who cannot speak French, German, Spanish or Chinese, most non-English speakers can speak and understand at least some English. The non-English language doorway page technique is a halfway solution to reaching non-English speaking people. A full method is discussed next.

Full Web Site Translation

The full translation of your Web site into foreign language(s) is a more thorough method of dealing with foreign markets. To get started doing this, you need to determine if it is worth doing. To find out where your product or service is wanted most in the world, you will need to undertake some market research into supply and demand for your service, product or information in various language markets.

Try www.marketresearch.com or www.mrs .org.uk and www.marketresearchworld.net for more information on doing market research and market researchers near you. This will require long hours spent searching various foreign language search engines with keywords and keyword phrases in the native language.

Next, determine what language the majority of your target market speaks. While you are at it also determine the target markets geographic, regional and cultural details. Now you are ready to decide whether it is worth your while to convert your site into other languages. In some cases it will not be sensible to provide foreign language translation.

Depending on the page count of your Web site, you may find that the cost of translation is prohibitive.

For instance if you are being charged $10 per page by your translation provider and you have 1,000 pages to translate, you may not have the $10,000 budget to complete the project. In this case you could look to translate a subset of your Web site using the content most likely to be of interest to the target foreign language market; and that will return to you the most sales (if your site is sales oriented).

Similarly, if after your research, you discover that the vast majority of sales of your service, product (or interest in the information your site provides), comes from the US and the UK markets, and the rest is evenly distributed among a large mix of foreign languages, you may decide it is not worth the translation and maintenance costs of creating a foreign language version of your Web site.

If you do decide after your research that there is a large enough market of non-English speakers, say Spanish language Internet users, you then need to decide how you will handle the Web site setup. For instance, do you want to host the site as a sub domain within your current Web site, i.e., http://es.currentwebdomain.com, or separately, i.e., www.currentwebdomain.es; where ".es" is the domain extension for Spain, and "currentwebdomain" is your current Web domain.

The two sites could reference each other and even share the same server space and thus use the same files and images where ever required.

Once you have decided on the domain setup for the new multi-lingual Web site, you then need to seek a translator proficient in Web site translation from your original language into your chosen foreign language(s). In some cases you may choose to support several languages, e.g., English, French, German, Spanish, Portuguese, Korean, Japanese, Arabic, Hebrew, Chinese, Swahili, etc.

Bear in mind that the more languages your Web site supports, the higher the costs of translation, implementation and maintenance. Furthermore, while implementation and maintenance costs could be quite linear in their increase with added supported languages, translation costs will vary wildly depending on the language(s) you choose to support.

It is a good idea to use a translation provider who also offers SEO services rather than a purely translation only service provider. This is because after your site is translated, the keyword and keyword phrases map may be dramatically changed and thus require SEO.

WARNING: Before giving the go ahead for all your Web pages to be translated and search engine optimized, have a home page and a few pages translated and optimized first. Check the effectiveness of the SEO on these pages by monitoring traffic to these sites for a trial period. If traffic to these pages is diabolically poor, you know not to waste any more money with your current multilingual SEO translator. Find someone who can get results.

This means you will need to apply SEO to the Web pages in the foreign languages after the translation. Save money and time and have the two activities carried out simultaneously. Search for "SEO multilingual translation" on any of the major search engines for a list of world class SEO translation service providers.

Your domain hosting service provider will most likely offer Web traffic monitoring services and facilities. However, wading through Web server logs can be a daunting and frustrating undertaking. There are many ways visitors come across or find your Web pages; this is not so obvious from all Web server logs.

You need to make sense of the data collected. Today, there are many people offering Web traffic monitoring services. You can also subscribe to a third party Web traffic monitoring service provider. Search for "Web traffic monitoring" on any major search engine for a list of service providers.

Chapter 3

Social Marketing Optimization

Social Marketing & Promotion

In this chapter we shall discuss the fuzzy marketing and promotion of your Web site, service, products or content via the rapidly growing social marketing medium. (Also see Social Networking; Appendix 1 for in-depth coverage of social networking Web sites). This chapter will cover syndicated news, forums, blogging, social community sites and social media sharing Web sites.

The social marketing phenomenon broke out of the 1990's Internet developmental years. During the proliferation of broadband usage which followed, social community sites sprung up to accommodate the growing Internet user base. Search engine optimizers required ways to utilize this new medium to market their Web sites, Web services and products and Web content. Social Media Optimization (SMO) was born. SMO is simply a set of methods for generating publicity through or from the Internet's social media. So, what are social media and online communities?

Social media is comprised of the online services and Web sites which offer Internet forums, message boards, Web logs (blogs), groups, Wikis (online collaboration tool for creating member or public edited information resources - in an encyclopedia style), vidcasts and podcasts (collection of digital media files distributed online for playback), news, pictures and video. Social media sites may utilize blogs, picture-sharing, vlogs (video blogs), wall-postings, e-mail, instant messaging, music-sharing, file sharing, group creation and voice over IP (Internet telephony), virtual worlds, etc. The vastness and complexity of SMO can be daunting and you can very easily get lost in the social media universe. Social media also changes rapidly, and the SMOs need to adapt fast to new changes, or quickly get left behind.

Some big players using and offering social media services are Google, Wikipedia, MySpace (social networking), Facebook (social networking), Last.fm (personal music), YouTube (social networking and video sharing), Second Life (virtual reality), Photobucket and Flickr (photo sharing).

Today, the importance of social media sites cannot be overstated. A quick look through the top global Web sites (http://alexa.com/site/ds /top_sites? ts_mode=global) finds the top ten contains ten social media sites; four of which are also search engines and the rest are either social networking sites such as MySpace, Facebook, Hi5 and Orkut; or social media sharing sites such as YouTube and the popular general reference site, one of which being Wikipedia.

You can see that social media sites are attracting the highest traffic on the Internet, so how can you benefit from this? We shall next delve into the various ways you can use SMO to improve popularity and visitor traffic to your Web site.

Reference Sites

The World Wide Web is a great place to find technical and educational information. Although some are privately hosted and require accounts and/or subscriptions, a large and growing amount of information sites have sprung up offering free access to information and knowledge. The database of information is growing to cover different media such as newsgroup posts, Web logs, video, music, sound files, software code and more.

Infosites

Infosite is a term I like to use for sites providing access to information and knowledge bases. Examples of these are encyclopedias, dictionaries, online libraries, maps, books, journals, magazines, news network postings, blogs, vlogs, and other archived non–interactive, non-editable (by users) information.

Microsoft for instance, has a huge database of support material and media in their knowledgebase accessible through http://support.microsoft.com. While you cannot directly interact with the knowledge base by editing it, you can comment on its usefulness in finding the answer to your problem or query.

Using Infosite Content

For SEO purposes you can use the information from infosites to create more keyword rich content for your own site. For instance, information from government sites can be used to add content to your own site, rather than linking to the government site alone. You can actually use SEO optimized versions of the content from the reference site.

Housing, Inland Revenue, law, law enforcement, medical, education and community information from government sites are a useful starting place. The good thing about most government site content is that it allows re-use, as in the case of Crown Copyrighted content from the UK government's Web sites.

WARNING: Always check the copyright statement and make sure you do not violate the infosites' copyright rules. Some infosites do not allow usage of their information without their permission. In such cases, I advise you to send an e-mail or letter to request permission before reusing their content.

Using Links

In the rare case that a highly ranked infosite allows voting, review comments, etc., relating to their content, you can submit reviews and comments where you somehow reference your Web site (either in the review or in the signature section if HTML links are allowed).

There are many tricks to this technique. You can either write a truly useful review or comment, or simply sign it, such as:

Samuel Blankson
http://www.samuelblankson.com

Or you can include a link in your comment, e.g., *"As an author at www.practicalbooks.org, I find that what this article said relates to—"*

You can: compare with your Web site, on where you first heard about the content being remarked upon (e.g., your Web site) and a whole host of other things. The important thing here is to do whatever is necessary to get your Web site name out there.

Keyword Boosting at Infosites

Most infosites do not allow or tolerate linking; therefore, you have to use a different approach with these. Find a keyword that is very unique to your site. In my case it is my name, "Samuel Blankson". By posting comments and reviews that have a unique keyword or keyword phrase mainly related to your Web site, you are helping to make that keyword more popular.

The more popular a keyword becomes, especially if it is referred back to your site, the more useful it is to you. Today "Samuel Blankson" is referred to 79,100 times on Google and 143,000 times on Yahoo!. And because my Web sites and products dominate the first SERPs, the majority of traffic related to that keyword will end up benefiting me. You can do the same thing for your Web site(s).

Today, infosites do not just give textual information as older versions did from the 1970's to early 1990's, now they cover other media also. The following are some examples of the diversity of infosites today:

- Computer software systems
  a) http://support.microsoft.com
  b) http://kbase.redhat.com
  c) http://support.esri.com/index.cfm?fa=knowledgeBase.
     gateway
- Government
  a) www.hmrc.gov.uk
  b) www.irs.gov
  c) https://www.cia.gov/library/publications/the-world-
     factbook/index.html

- Finance
  a) www.investopedia.com
- Education
  a) http://kb.iu.edu
  b) www.law.cornell.edu
- Internet
  a) http://kb.mozillazine.org/Knowledge_Base
  b) http://kbase.info.apple.com
  c) www.oscommerce.info
  d) www.icthubknowledgebase.org.uk
  e) www.tkb.org
- Films
  a) www.imdb.com
- Music
  a) www.onlinemusicdatabase.com
  b) www.allmusic.com
  c) www.sing365.com
- Computer Games
  a) www.games-db.com
- News Archives
  a) http://news.google.com
- Maps
  a) http://maps.live.com
  b) http://maps.google.com
- Images
  a) http://images.google.com
  b) www.fotosearch.com
- Books
  a) http://isbndb.com
  b) http://books.google.com
  c) http://onlinebooks.library.upenn.edu
  d) www.amazon.com

Use any search engine to look for infosites. A search query of "*[topic you are interested in] database*" or "*[topic you are interested in] knowledgebase*", should yield the desired results. Remove these characters "[]", including the quotation marks, otherwise the search term will be treated as a phrase, i.e., "address database" will be treated as: find all pages with the exact term *"address database"*, rather than, find all pages with the keywords address and database.

Concerning non-text media, all the large search engines are now indexing images, sound and video. Therefore it makes sense to properly tag (or provide descriptive, optimized keywords, description or names) for your images, sound and video files. Similarly, if you create software code, make sure it is also properly tagged. Without proper tagging, your images, video and sound will be lost to search engines. As an example, instead of calling a music file "1.mpg", try something more descriptive, like *Micheal_Jackson-Thriller.mpg*.

Don't just stop there, in the details tags of the file, include the following: title, subtitle, comments, artists, album, year, genre, length, bit rate, publisher, author URL, copyright, parental rating, etc. The richer the details are the more likely it will be found by someone looking for related details. Pay close attention to title, subtitle, comment and author URL; these are vital.

Wikis

A Wiki is a piece of software. Wikis allow users to collaborate through creating, editing and linking Web pages. Wikis have grown to be very popular and today there are thousands of corporate and private Wikis, and even more online Wikis. The largest Wiki is Wikipedia although Google has its eyes set on overtaking Wikipedia with www.wiki.com, which allows users to add Wikis, start up new Wikis and search various Wikis (including Wikipedia and independent Wikis), or all of them.

It is important to remember that as www.wiki.com grows in popularity, having a Wiki of your own which is accessible through the others, will become critical for SMO benefits. This is because the default option to search on www.wiki.com is "all wikis". This means your Wiki has a good chance to be featured in the SERPs, if it covers a search term in great enough detail, and is relevant.

If you have not done so already visit Wikipedia and see what they offer, then go to wiki.com and setup your own Wiki. Populate it with information relevant to your Web site content and topic. Be specific and focus mainly on what your site does or covers best. Make the content in-depth and highly useful. You can provide loads of links to your site throughout the Wiki pages.

Make sure you opt for the hosted Wiki service offered by wiki.com rather than hosting it on your own Web site. This is because the wiki.com domain is most likely better ranked than your Web page. You can also opt to install the Wiki on a separate domain and host it from there. Choose this option if you have the technical knowledge to install, configure and manage it, the funds to maintain and upgrade it, and the Wiki hosting domain has a higher rank than your Web site.

Remember, the Wiki will grow in size and if you host it yourself, you may find that your Web space is inadequately sized to accommodate future growth. This will require more money to be spent on Web space leasing or extra hard drives.

You can submit updates to pages on public Wikis (or if you are a member, private Wikis). In most Wikis, the updates can include HTML links, therefore you could include links to your Web site in your Wiki updates; however, if your edits are non-helpful, inaccurate and your links are inappropriate, blatant attempts at link advertising or out of topic, they most likely will be replaced by a better Wiki entry or deleted.

Remember, as with most SEO and SMO, you have to give something valuable or at least give something perceived to be useful in order to be allowed to take (i.e., to be allowed to promote your Web page/Web site link). You can also promote keywords and keyword phrases that are specific to your Web site in your Wiki updates. This is especially effective when the keywords or keyword phrases are trademarks, unique names or part of your Web site name.

Discussion Sites

Discussion boards partially originated from the BBS, (Bulletin Board System) used in Berkeley, California. The earliest form used hardwired terminals in close knit neighborhoods. The technology and concept did not take off until the late 1970's when the ability to connect computers via the telephone line allowed BBSes to span larger geographic areas and be accessed by larger groups of users.

Bulletin Boards

Those early BBSes allowed users to upload and download files, hold synchronous discussions and exchange news by dialing into a central BBS computer via slow dial up modems. Due to the speed restrictions at the time it took a while before images, sound and video files were regularly exchanged. The BBSes grew to be very popular in the early 1990s. At that time BBSes offered e-mail, messaging, access to the Internet through gateways, and rampant file sharing.

The proliferation of the Internet and access speeds caused BBSes to fall in popularity and usage. The largest BBS at the time, FidoNET, is still active now and can be accessed at www.fidonet.org. It comprises over 10,000 nodes or computer systems forming the Fidonet BBS network. Still accessible via dialup, it has the added benefit of also being fully accessible via the Internet, however, only file upload and download, e-mail and news is supported.

Due to the requirement of dialing into a BBS system via the phone line, long distance and international usage of BBSes was limited by telephone costs. Although Internet gateways allowed BBSes to gain more functionality and reach through newsgroups and e-mail, the restrictive speeds and lack of asynchronous real-time, rich textured media interaction caused them to almost be replaced by the Internet and more modern social media sites of today. BBS systems are still used in companies for conferencing systems, in communities, local groups and throughout the Internet.

Internet users far out number BBS users today, making it not worth your while marketing specifically to BBS users.

Furthermore, most BBS users also use the Internet while the vast majority of Internet users have never heard of the BBS before.

If you use BBSes and want to know how you can promote your Web site within the BBS network, you simply have to keep the following in mind. As a user, BBSes allow you to send text e-mails, receive text e-mails, receive news, post discussions, and upload and download files. Those are the restrictions of the medium. Add to that, BBSes are often closed networks, heavily monitored, and often dedicated to specific topics, and you may find that their communities can be tight-knit.

Therefore, if you plan on sending bulk e-mails, software generated discussion posts or flood their bandwidth with large binary (non-text) files, you may get banned. The best you can do is to provide useful and/or informative discussion or newsgroup posts with your "message" and your Web site details within your post or in the signature. It is normally better to develop some trust at the forum first by contributing to various discussions.

Bulletin board systems today generally offer members access to news postings via a global, decentralized discussion network called Usenet. Usenet was established in 1980 and allowed users to post their comments, questions and subscribe to the Usenet's one or more relevant newsgroups. Another way to make the BBS members aware of your Internet service is to generate news worthy press releases that target the type of news normally featured in the relevant groups subscribed to by the BBS. This is a less direct approach and its effectiveness will be hard to measure, as the news will be read by more BBS and Internet users than just members of the targeted BBS.

You could also develop a useful software or file which you upload to the BBS for others to download. This software or file would have to be relevant to the board topic and somehow market your Internet Web site when executed, used or shut down. A message such as, *"This free software was brought to you by www.yourwebsite.com. Visit us for more free stuff"*.

Message Boards

Message boards offer similar functionality to the BBS. The main difference is that they are accessible by anyone who has Internet access, a Web browser, and in some cases an account. Some message boards allow posting of messages without an account, while most require you to create an account first, before you are allowed access.

On a message board, members discuss topics with subsequent posts to the discussion "daisy chained" to the previous posting. Members are often allowed to start up new discussion chains (threads), and in some forums starting up a new thread gives you administrative rights over that thread, allowing you to censor, delete posts, or in some cases, elevate posts to the top of the chain.

Message boards are also called Web forums, or discussion groups. They can facilitate clubs, or even support online communities. They are very useful to SEO for two main reasons; firstly, they can help improve your page rank at search engines if you can get your link displayed within your posts, and secondly, you can promote your Web site directly or indirectly through the topic under discussion. The largest message boards can be found at the following Web sites:

- http://groups.google.com
- http://groups.yahoo.com
- www.big-boards.com
- www.microsoft.com/communities/newsgroups/en-us

There are a few message board etiquettes to observe. To avoid being banned, never post multiple copies of the exact same post in different message boards. Avoid posting multiple copies of the same message within the same message board or worse within the same thread.

Read the message board rules carefully before starting to post messages, and try to adhere to them as best as you can. The best way way to use message boards is to start a thread that will discuss a topic which your Web site can predominantly feature, or ask a question that can only be answered with the link to your Web site.

If you want to enter a busy thread and promote your site, choose a message board which allows HTML code or BBcode. Then insert your Web site address within your signature when setting up your message board account.

Any comment you make on the message board will then have your signature appended and thus your site link is promoted.

For message boards that do not allow BBcode or Web links, you will have to spend a little more time to build up a discussion or build your status within a popular thread. Make sure the discussion has scope for promotion or mentioning your Web site at some stage to support the argument or discussion.

If you can start or steer a discussion, wholly about your Web site, that is even better. Be careful though, if the thread turns negative towards your site you could lose some of the promotional benefits. If this happens you will still keep the page rank benefits from the links.

Bookmarking

Before we move onto more modern social media, let's look at the topic of social bookmarking and its significance to SMO. The following is a list of bookmarking and conversation tracking sites:

- http://blinklist.com
- http://bookmarks.yahoo.com
- http://del.icio.us
- http://digg.com
- http://reddit.com
- www.facebook.com
- www.google.com/bookmarks
- www.livejournal.com
- www.newsvine.com
- www.stumbleupon.com

You can also visit www.addthis.com/bookmark.php for more social bookmarking sites.

Addthis.com offers reliable and free widgets that simplify the addition and use of social bookmarking on your sites, blogs and feeds. Their widgets are easy to install and makes your implementation of social bookmarking uncluttered and professional. Furthermore, addthis.com provides useful, free statistics on how visitors are treating your Web site and feeds. Using social bookmarking makes a lot of sense for the following reasons:

1) Makes it easy for visitors on your site to bookmark your content and subscribe to your feeds.
2) Helps send your Web site content to social bookmarking providers. This allows traffic to be directed to you.
3) The increased links to your site increases your link popularity, and thus your page rank.

As you execute your social marketing plan, you will generate and create many links to Web sites, video clips, sound clips, articles, Web logs, etc. It can get very confusing and frustrating having to remember what these Web sites were and what they were related to. Social bookmarking sites solve this problem by allowing you to bookmark links you want to store as you browse social bookmark supporting Web sites.

You can also organize and categorize your social bookmarked links so that you can find them quickly and make better sense of your Web usage. Most social bookmarking sites also allow you to share these links with other social bookmarking sites and Web sites that support them.

Every Web page you want to allow visitors to promote and spread across the Internet for you should have a social bookmarking widget imbedded in it, as should every article, press release, video feed, news feed, video picture or mobile blog that you upload.

Logs/Diaries

The Internet diary, journal or scrap book is a medium for people to voice their opinions or simply keep a one sided record of their daily lives. Today the Web log or blog and video log or vlog community, is growing fast. Blogs are diary type entries written by Internet users. These sites are similar to discussion forums, with one significant difference. The posts are one way, from the author and owner of the blog. Every one else can only read what is written.

Some blogs allow readers to comment on what is written or review it; however, depending upon the blog site, readers may or may not be able to add to the blogs.

Blogging can be time intensive and to be successful at it normally requires you to present some level of intimacy of your activities, thoughts and opinions. It almost seems that the more radical and controversial your blogs are, the more likely you will attract a good audience. Celebrities who already have an established audience can get a head start attracting blog traffic. You can search for different genres of blogs using the search engines, but here are a few top blogging sites to consider:

- Blog Sites
  a) http://www.youtube.com/blog
  b) www.blogged.com
  c) www.blogger.com
  d) www.blogspot.com
  e) www.freeblogit.com
  f) www.wordpress.com
- Business
  a) www.b5media.com
- Search Engines
  a) http://blogsearch.google.com
  b) www.technorati.com/blogs/directory

There are basically three ways of making money with blogs: advertising, endorsement and repackaging.

Advertising

It is easy to understand advertising. Advertisers are always interested in buying advertisement space where large volumes of people congregate or pass through. The Internet is no different. If you write blogs or plan to, make sure you allow advertisers to advertise on your blog. You can simplify the placement of advertisements on your blog site by using banner advertisements, or contextual advertising such as Google AdWords.

We will cover Google's advertising services in another chapter. Through banners, affiliation links and Google AdWords, you can generate money from the traffic visiting your blog pages. By clicking the links to exit your blog site, your visitors literally generate cash for you. This cash is paid by the advertiser and can be earned per click on their advertisement or per purchase made from the visitor at the advertisers' site. Your account is automatically credited due to a tracking code in the advertisement. This informs the advertiser where the customer was sent from (i.e., your Web site, etc.). The following are some sites for promotion and advertisment of your blog:

Web Polls

• www.vizu.com

Advertising

• http://shoppingads.com
• www.bidvertiser.com
• www.feedburner.com
• www.kontera.com
• www.problogger.net
• www.text-link-ads.com

Endorsement

Let's look at the second way of making money with blogs, endorsements and affiliations. The main way money is made on the Web is through product and service endorsements. When your blog becomes popular, your fans will be a great source of income for you. There are many companies that pay bloggers to endorse their products and services. Simply by endorsing products and services within your blogs or on your blog site, or any Web site for that matter, you can be paid by the companies that manufacture these products or offer these services.

Today there are affiliate programs for almost every product or service you can imagine. Simply search for *"affiliate program [the topic, service or product of interest] [your country]"* on a major search engine and you will find hundreds of affiliate programs. We shall revisit affiliates again in more details in page 111, but for now, I hope you can understand the value of making money from your blog site.

Repackaging

The third way of making money from your blog is to repackage the contents and create a new product that you can then sell separately. The most popular product created from repackaging blog posts is books. Yes, you can take all your blog posts, organize them into a book and publish this. You can then advertise the book on your blog site for sale to your blog readers.

If you are already published or can easily secure a publisher to publish the book, then that is great. However, even if you do not have a publisher and cannot guarantee finding one that will agree to publish your book quickly enough, you can turn to the many print on demand publishers available today. Try any of the following:

- www.booksurge.com
- www.cafepress.com
- www.google.com

Offering online book publishing services, these book companies offer simple tools to help you publish your book and get it available in online bookstores; as well as being available to order your book from libraries and shops.

The process for publishing your book will vary from each provider, therefore visit their site, read their frequently asked questions and speak with their staff.

Photo-Blogging and Mo-Blogging

Photo-blogging is similar to blogging; however it centers on photographs rather than text, as in blogging. Text is used to enhance and give added detail to the images, while maintaining the images as the main focus. Photo-blog sites allow syndication of photo-blogs through RSS or Atom. This allows the images to be delivered directly via the transmission medium as soon as any new image is added to the photo-blog.

Mo-blogs are photo-blogs with images and video uploaded directly from the mobile phone to the mo-blog site. The owner then sorts the images, tags them and adds text via the Web site. Again, these mo-blogs can be syndicated and subscribed to, just as a news feed and whenever a new image is added, it is distributed to the subscribers.

Apart from being a medium for exchanging, sharing and displaying your photographs, photo-blogging and mo-blogging can actually be a source of income when used correctly. A photographer for instance, can generate a lot of interest in his talent and photography stock by uploading a new photo every day to a photo-blog site.

In the case of mo-blogging, you could use images from your mobile phone camera to diary your dating experiences and use the mo-blog to promote your dating Web site. Or, you could use the mo-blog to diary your training and preparation for a major sporting event to raise money for a charity. People following your progress via the photo-blog or mo-blog would be encouraged to go to your donation Web site and donate money to the charity in support of your efforts. The usage options are limitless. Even a trader could use images to show his trading progress in order to promote a Web site or seminar on trading.

Make sure in the photo-blog account, you have a link to your main Web site which hosts all your images. The main Web site could also highlight your full services offered and any products such as framed images and photo books, etc.

It is also advantageous to attach your name and Web site address to each picture you upload, so that as it travels around the Internet and viewers know where to go for more.

Similarly in your photo-blog, write interesting labels and associated text to each image. In photo-blogs, the image says more than the text, however the text can be used to arouse more interest in your Web site.

You can run your own photo-blog on your Web site, however you probably will get more SEO value from having a www.flickr.com or www.fotolog.com account. Visit the following sites for more photo-blogging services:

- http://blogs.msdn.com/pix
- http://phlog.net
- www.fotothing.com
- www.photoblogs.org

Video Logs (or Vlogs)

Vlogs are the video equivalent of blogging, similar to photo-blogging but with video and sound. Vlogging gained popularity during the 1980's due in part to the BBC, and recently due to Google's YouTube and the many vlog sites that are rapidly growing.

To quickly get started vlogging, you simply need a digital video camera, webcam or even a mobile phone with a built-in video camera and connection to your Internet enabled computer. If you want to produce more advanced and professional video (which is not necessarily required to make money with vlogs), you can purchase a teleprompter, and software for adding backdrops and effects to your recordings.

Search for *"Teleprompter"*, *"video backdrop"*, *"video editing software"* and *"video effects"* or *"professional video editing software"* on Google. You will be surprised by how much free, quality software can be downloaded to help you add professionalism to your vlog productions. The following are vlog production and playback software sites:

- Camstudio— www.camstudio.org
- Final Cut Pro—by Apple:
  www.apple.com/finalcutstudio/finalcutpro
- iMovie— by Apple: www.apple.com/ilife/imovie
- Jing— by the Jing Project: www.jingproject.com
- Moviemaker—by Microsoft:
  www.microsoft.com/windowsxp/downloads/updates/movi emaker2.mspx
- Vlog It— by Adobe: www.adobe.com/products/vlogit

Some vlog sites also offer video editing facilities via their Web site. See the following for examples:

- www.im.tv/vlog
- www.motionbox.com

The following is a list of useful vlog related Web sites. Most of them offer free uploads of your vlog onto their vlog server. Many also offer you the ability to tag properly and also allow social bookmarking of your vlog. A few of them allow you to syndicate your vlog via RSS as news feed; allowing subscribers to receive new uploads automatically.

Free

- http://blip.tv
- http://crackle.com
- http://freevlog.org
- http://mefeedia.com
- http://photobucket.com
- http://uncutvideo.aol.com/Main.do
- http://video.google.com
- http://video.msn.com/video.aspx?mkt=en-gb
- http://video.yahoo.com
- www.blinkx.com
- www.flixya.com
- www.metacafe.com
- www.revver.com
- www.veoh.com
- www.videocasting-station.com
- www.vidlogs.com
- www.vimeo.com
- www.youtube.com

Help

- www.node101.org

The following links are vlog sites that specifically aim to help vloggers earn an income from vlogging:

Business

- http://adhoc.blinkx.com
- www.thevideosense.com

Opt-in RSS to Mail Subscription

- http://vlogdir.com service
- www.livevideo.com

Map Locations of Vloggers

- http://vlogmap.org

Directories

- http://videoblogging-universe.com/vlogs
- www.01vlog.com
- www.videopodcasts.tv
- www.youcandoitpublishing.com

Social Networking Sites

- www.bebo.com
- www.facebook.com
- www.myspace.com
- www.twitter.com

Tutorials

- http://community.vlogmap.org/handbook
- www.oreillynet.com/pub/a/oreilly/digitalmedia/2005/07/2 7/vloghtml

Social Networking

MySpace, Facebook, Hi5 and Orkut are all social networking Web sites which have grown to be very popular. As we saw earlier, these sites now dominate the top ten with the highest traffic, next to the search engines on the Internet. How can SMO help draw some of that traffic to your Web site?

Let us look at what these social networking sites actually do. They allow you to build popularity through your own friends and associates. However, it doesn't stop there. This is because friends of your friends can also see your account (if you allow them), and thus your network of friends can grow and spiral from these extended friendships and associates.

You can upload pictures, videos, write and post in blogs, fan clubs, groups and discussion forums, comment on other peoples content, forward content to your friends (others can also do the same to your content), run polls and subscribe to special applets which give you more opportunity to attract attention. You can also create events and invite people to them as well as host other services and features.

Finally, you can place pay-per-click or pay-per-display advertisements or feeds on your site. Feeds are syndicated through RSS or Atom, and are displayed on a social network site to all subscribers.

The list of features, effectiveness and functionality varies slightly from one social networking site to the other. It is difficult to maintain accounts effectively on more than one unless that is your full time job. To get started, I suggest signing up with the top five social networking sites to determine which one you prefer. Do not upload all your friends' contact details to all five. This will upset some people and it also might cause problems for you down the line when they decide to stick to one, which you do not prefer.

While you should make one or two social networking sites your base, you can promote your content across the full list of social networking sites. In fact, even if you did nothing but provide a popular post, it would soon travel around all the social networking sites anyway.

The following is a list of the top five social networking sites offering general social networking services:

1. Facebook: www.facebook.com
2. Friendster: www.friendster.com
3. MySpace: www.myspace.com
4. Orkut–(Google owned): www.orkut.com
5. Spaces Central–(Microsoft owned): http://spaces.live.com

Also See Social Networking; Appendix 1, for a list of the other social networking Web sites. If the Web site you want to promote using SMO covers a niche topic, or is in a foreign language, you can target social networking sites that specifically cater to that audience. The services offered by social networking sites differ widely, making the SMO applications differ from site to site.

Adding to this, the effectiveness of SMO at any one social networking site changes regularly as their competitors add new functionality and services. Because of this, we shall look at how different features of social networking sites can be utilized for SMO purposes.

Tagging

For a media file to be searchable, it has to be assigned keywords and terms. This is *tagging*. Without proper tagging your media file will be lost on the Internet to social networkers. Sites such as www.tagworld.com specialize in tagging, however most social networking sites allow manual tagging of media files. Use tags that will guarantee the most frequent usage. Research the most popular keywords before assigning tags to your social media files.

File Storage and Hosting

You cannot always place all your social media files in your social networking account profile, therefore you need to store larger files somewhere else and link to them. There are a host of sites offering this service for free, with most offering storage of over 100MB per file.

If you need to store really large files or just a lot of files such as an entire archive of video clips, sound files, blogs or other text based media , etc., you should consider using a file storage facility.

Image and Video Editing Tools

It is necessary to edit your images and video files to make them more interesting and compelling. To do this, simply add your Web site name to the beginning, the credits, the end or a back drop, etc. (which is a very good idea by the way). You will need to either purchase or download from the Internet, install, configure and learn to use new software.

Alternatively, you could find a Web site that offered this service for free, and use their tools and support facilities to create, edit and publish your media files. *See* Appendix 3 Video Sharing Sites, for a list of these Web sites; www.jumpcut.com is a great place to start your search.

Video Streaming

Adding video clips enhances your social media Web site. Whenever possible, automate the viewing of your media files by streaming the images. Streaming your video media files is always a good idea. It means your viewers can watch the videos immediately from your social networking site without requiring an installation of extra software. Streaming also puts an end to slow download times and compatibility issues for your viewers.

You can add your files to sites that will stream them for you such as www.youtube.com. *See* Appendix 3 Video Sharing Sites for a list of other streaming media sites. On the social networking site, simply place a link to the streaming media or add the code to enable this.

Blogging, Photo-Blogging and Vlogging

As we discovered earlier, blogs, photo-blogs and vlogs are great tools for promoting your Web site, building a fan base and monetizing your content. Nowadays, most social networking sites accommodate blogging, photo-blogging and vlogging; however the functionality, features and effectiveness for capitalization will vary between them.

You may need to host your blogs, vlogs and photo-blogs at another site and link to them from your preferred social networking site. Do this if your preferred social networking site does not offer the best services, functions and tools such as comments, reviews, polls, syndication, tagging and capitalization. Include social bookmarking links wherever possible.

Also See Niche Social Networking; Appendix 1 for examples of niche social networking sites, such as Live Journal (www.livejournal.com), Flickr (www.flickr.com) and Blogger (www.blogger.com), etc.

Advertising and Google Adwords

Some social networking sites offer you the opportunity to capitalize on your content through advertising. Normally this is achieved with a Google AdWords type of pay-per-click (PPC) program, or site targeted advertising.

PPC advertising is where you create an advertisement (normally either a banner or text advertisement), and elect to pay a small, set fee, for directed relevant traffic. Each time a visitor clicks on your advertisement you are charged for it. Thus you pay-per-click. PPC advertisements are normally displayed on the service providers' Web site such as Google's search pages, or in the case of social networking sites, on their pages.

The advertisements are published on pages whose content appear to contain relevant references to what the advertiser has specified as keywords and keyword phrases of interest for the advertisement.

In the case of site targeted traffic: advertisers bid on a cost-per-impression (CPI) basis, whenever their advertisements are displayed on Web sites that are relevant to their elected keywords and keyword phrases. Again, they can select banner ads or text ads. With CPI you are paying for the amount of times your advertisement appears on pages, rather than for clicks on your advertisement.

On social networking sites PPC is preferred over CPI although both may be offered by the social networking site.

How can you make money with PPC or CPI? In this book there is an entire chapter dedicated to this topic, *See page 94.* Therefore, in this section we will briefly cover the topic.

When you create a blog, vlog, photo-blog, article, podcast, mo-blog, event, fan club, group, forum, social networking profile page, product, service, Web site or any other creation, you can also make a PPC advertisement to get your message out, and get noticed. Some social networking sites even track ads associated with syndicated content.

On social networking sites, you can specify how much you are prepared to pay-per-click or per impression. Then you add a title for your advertisement, descriptive text, images, Web site and media file links, video, discussion groups, forums, comments, polls, e-mail address(es) and other means of contact, (Google offers the click-to-call service which enables visitors to call the advertiser through Google), error reporting links, review links, social bookmarking links, voting links and 'tell a friend' links.

Not all social networking site's PPC programs allow inclusion of all the tools listed above. However, all social networking sites that provide PPC or CPI services allow a subset of the points listed above.

By the way, if you are creating an advertisement for your Web site through Google AdWords, you could have the advertisement link to a landing page that uses all these devices to maximize the effectiveness of the advertisement campaign.

A major advantage that PPC and CPI advertising have over conventional offline advertisements, is that they are cheap, they allow you to control your budget and you get immediate feedback through results. Therefore, you can tweak your advertisement to improve the results through the life cycle of the advertisement campaign.

A last point about monitoring the effectiveness of your advertisement campaign is that most PPC and CPI providers supply useful statistics on the demography, time, source, quality of clicks and your advertisement campaign in general. This is useful data to base your tweaking on.

For instance, if your advertisement campaign is proving more successful in a particular country, you may want to focus your advertisement campaign on that country and exclude the other parts of the world where you are acheiving little or no interest.

Similarly, if your advertisement is proving more effective during a certain time of the day, this could help you tweak the advertisement to apply more to the unpopular times. You could also identify interest groups you never thought of prior to submitting the advertisement campaign.

Polling

Audience interaction is a good way for retaining visitors to your site. Giving people the ability to voice their opinion on an interesting or controversial topics will get more visitors staying longer on your Web pages, than having no interactive options at all.

Polls give you a way of getting views and opinions from your audience. Add polls to your social networking pages with polling sites such as www.vizu.com or *See* Appendix 6 Polling Sites, for more information.

There are several ways to benefit from polls; firstly create new polls and secondly use existing polls. There are benefits to both.

Creating new polls allows you to gather relevant research data from visitors about what they think of your content. You can also create a poll on every polling site you can get to, asking what people think about your Web site. This will spread your Web link and thus help your Web page rank due to the back-linking, and might get more traffic to your site from the polling sites.

Additionally, using pre-existing polls allows you to select polls that have proven to be highly effective in the past. If you can attach your Web site link to the poll e.g., "*by www.practicalbooks.org*" or "*by practicalbooks.org*". You can also post polls into other people's social networking pages through HTML codes. This will help promote your Web site address and drive traffic to your site.

Some polling sites also pay you to poll for them. This is a useful way to use the traffic passing through your Web site to make money.

Finally, polls can be useful in providing you with your visitors' opinions on your service and Web content. Place a poll with each blog, attached media file or information page to collect research data for free.

Forums

We have already discussed forum usage for SEO, the techniques are the same for SMO. If your social networking site offers a forum feature, you can apply the methods discussed earlier by creating your own forum and discussing topics; which promote your Web site(s), affiliations, endorsements, blogs, vlogs and other social media.

Similarly, you can also utilize other people and other groups' forums to great effect; advertising your Web page links either in your posts or in the signature of your posts and promoting your other social media. As all your social media should be tagged and helping to drive traffic to your site, it also helps to advertise your social media. Include social bookmarking links wherever possible.

Groups

With groups on social networking (as is true for groups anywhere else), you need to post regularly and be involved in hot topics to get the greatest benefit. If HTML is allowed in the group posts, make sure yours links back to your Web site. You can also promote your social media links, files and profiles, as well as your Web site, within your group posts. Include social bookmarking links wherever possible.

Favorites Lists

Some social networking sites allow members to add people's profiles, groups, forums, blogs, Web links, media links, news, feeds and more. While this feature is useful for you to store places, links and people you want to refer to in the future, the tool can also be great for SEO if the site allows you to make the favorites accessible by the public.

If the latter is true, i.e., the social networking site allows you to publish your favorites, then make sure your favorites contain all links that lead to promotion of your Web site, including your URL.

Events

Some social networking sites such as Facebook.com and MySpace.com allow members to post events. This is a social tool that allows you to create a type of group media. However, it is related to some event in the future or a recurring event, e.g., a weekly club night, birthday party, or a product launch party, etc.

You can use this feature to publicize launches, new additions to your Web site, branch openings, etc., and any other event you can use to promote your site. Always have a link to your site and attach as much media such as video clips and pictures, as well as text to the event.

When people sign up for the event, make sure you keep them posted with updates and regular promotional information relating to the event and your site.

E-mail

E-mail advertising is a controversial topic. No one likes to receive unsolicited e-mail (junk mail or spam), therefore make sure you do not send spam. Only send e-mail to people who have already agreed to receive e-mail from you or your Web site, blog, forum, etc.

With a quality list of opt-in e-mail addresses, you can market directly to people who you already know have an interest in what you are sending them. There are many ways of acquiring opt-in e-mail addresses; you can obtain them from your blogs, forums, groups and Web sites. You can also get them from polls and comments posted about your media files or Web sites.

If you have something you are giving for free, you could make it a prerequisite that downloaders supply their e-mail addresses, and a reply confirmation via e-mail; before making the download available to them. This is useful if you are supplying a Web applet or application. You could also use this technique for the download of music, video and images (not samples).

Over time, you will amass a large database of e-mail addresses. Send regular updates, promotions and seasonal greetings to the opt-in e-mail subscribers. They are a great source of repeat business and ongoing promotion. You can use polls in the e-mails; *See* Appendix 6 Polling Sites or http://polldaddy.com for further details.

Use social media and social networking Web site tools to give the opt-in e-mail subscribers media that they can share, pass on to friends, and comment about in their social network profiles; always making sure your Web site link is included.

> **WARNING:** Make sure your visitors are aware that you are harvesting their e-mail addresses and acquire their consent before proceeding. This is called opt-in e-mail; it means they have consented to you using their e-mail address for the purpose(s) you stated in the consent agreement.

Where you do not control the e-mail addresses, or they are hidden from you as is the case in most social media sites, you can still send people your site link. By using humorous, controversial or interesting media files and links, stories, reports, articles, forum posts, etc., it is easier to send promotional material en-masse. Using the internal messaging service of the soicial networking site, you can send such e-mails to your network of friends and their network of friends.

Recommendations and Reviews

Recommendations are endorsements given by visitors or friends to your Web site or social network profile. They do this using a 'recommendation to a friend' link and supply the e-mail address(es) of their friend(s). This is different from a review. A review is a written recommendation posted to your social network profile or Web site about a social media file or post of yours.

Others who view the page, post or media file will see the attached comment and can also add their own comment. People like to comment on things that are popular; therefore the more comments you receive on one of your postings or media files, the more others will want to add their comments.

Make sure you post and add media worth commenting on by your viewers. You can re-use other people's media files as posts, so long as there are no copyright issues. Check first that the copyright allows sharing of the media file or post before using on your social network profile.

Comments create a buzz and increase traffic to your profile. Similarly you can add your comments to other people's popular posts or social media. Make sure you include your Web site address in the signature of the recommendation, comment or review, e.g., *"by Samuel Blankson – www.samuel blankson.com"*.

As your comment, review or recommendation makes the rounds through the social networks; your site will be back-linked on other sites and thus help with your page rank and increase your Web site traffic.

> **WARNING:** Do not abuse the voting system in an attempt to make an unpopular media item more popular by artificially raising its votes. When visitors see the unfairness in your voting system, they will most likely stop using the voting facility, and you may lose them forever.

Votes

Some social networking Web sites allow visitors to vote on content. Typically, a voting system of slide bars, '1' to '5' or 'very useful' to 'not useful', is used. Votes can help you to see what content on your social networking profile is popular and what is not. You can then replace the unpopular links, media files and posts with more popular ones.

Fine tuning your content in this manner will greatly improve your social networking profile's popularity. The links to your Web site from there will receive more visitors. You can also use the power of votes on your own Web site.

Classified

Some social networking sites offer a classified section. Generally this is a free to use facility that allows members to post items for sale or advertise services. Most free classifieds tend to be abused by link boosters. Their usefulness for promoting your Web site may be limited due to this.

That said, a well written and interesting advertisement can attract the right type of interest from classifieds. Make sure you utilize this free service to advertise your Web site wherever it is provided. You can make your classified advertisement more interesting with media links and even a poll.

Preferences (books, music, movies, etc.)

Social networking success is based entirely on popularity. Therefore, to increase your status, you have to associate with Web sites, content and media files that are popular. Similarly, associating with in-style music, books, movies, games and anything else that is currently very trendy, will improve your popularity (even if slightly).

With that in mind, utilize the preferences tool offered by social networking Web sites. This tool offers members the ability to specify what they are currently "into", such as what you are listening, reading, playing (games), enjoying (holidays), and/or watching (movies, etc).

A little research will tell you what is currently popular in all these categories. Go to your favorite downloadable site and download music, books and games and try them out. You never know, if they are very popular there might be something useful in them. Now you can also say you are listening, reading, playing and watching the most popular things on the Web.

Widgets

A widget is a small piece of software that gives your profile added functionality. Software developers create these applets for social networking sites for many reasons; promotion of their skills, business or simply for fun.

To find already popular widgets for your social networking profile, search for *"widgets [name of your social networking site]"* on any major search engine, e.g., "widget Facebook".

Microsoft's release of Popfly on its new Silverlight platform (www.popfly.com), promises to change how applications are developed and by whom. Popfly pledges to give anyone the tool to create vibrant widgets to enhance social networking profiles. Search for *"Creating a Popfly Video Mashup[1]"* on http://video.msn.com, and you will see an example of how simple this tool is to use.

Using the tool or a similar widget creation tool, you can create a simple widget that helps promote your Web site. You can learn to create widgets and distribute them through your social networking site, Web site, blog, forum and group posts. In fact, distributing a cool widget hosted on your Web site is a sure way to drive traffic to your site.

Once your friends see and use the widget, they will want to have it on their own social networking profile. Thus, the widget will spread, taking with it your Web site's popularity and it will increase your Web traffic.

Microsoft's Popfly is not the only tool for widget creation, try www.dapper.net, www.widgetbox.com or search for "widget tools" and "mashup tools" on one of the top five search engines. Create a widget from your blogs, images, videos, vlogs, and Web site content or simply create a mashup of other people's data and share it with the world.

Media Subscription

Web syndication is making a portion or page of your Web site or Web content available for others to use. This is normally read by an aggregator or a feed reader. Feed readers can also allow you to subscribe to syndicated feeds. When new data is added to the feed, the feed reader downloads and makes it available to you to read, listen, see and/or use.

---

[1] A mashup is a Web application that combines data from more than one source into a single integrated tool.

Most social networking sites allow their content to be syndicated via Atom or RSS (Really Simple Syndication)—the two main syndication standards. RSS was developed first. Atom was developed later to overcome some of RSS's shortcomings. However, RSS is by far the most popular and supported standard.

Feeds contain entries such as headline, excerpts, summaries, articles, links to Web content and XML tags. It is important to understand that your media files will not be transmitted by the syndication system. Only links, text and tags will be transmitted. This allows the bandwidth required for syndication to remain relatively small.

Once you syndicate a blog, vlog, Web page or regularly updated content, a feed is created and visitors can subscribe to that feed. When you add new content, the user's feed reader detects the change in content and fetches the details of the new addition. It then feeds this to the subscriber, allowing them to access the data.

You don't have to visit individual Web sites looking for feeds to sign up to them. You can search for topics of interest and feeds which have been tagged with the relevant keywords. Google, Yahoo! and Microsoft Live all supply readers for RSS or Atom. Find them on the Yahoo! directory. Search for *"RSS readers and aggregators in the Yahoo! Directory"* on any search engine or visit the following link: http://dir.yahoo.com/Computers_and_Internet/Data_Formats/ XML__eXtensible_Markup_Language_/RSS/RSS_Readers_a nd_Aggregators.

You can subscribe to feeds using an aggregator or feed reader such as Google Reader. While subscription to feeds is great, creation of them is even better. We shall look more closely at RSS syndication next. In the mean time, remember to use the syndication feature/service offered by your social networking provider.

To allow your feed to be better indexed and thus more searchable, title your feeds with important search terms. Tag your feeds using the XML tags provided. If you can get at the XML code, add tag data directly to the XML code. Use link text to emphasize keywords and use full link locations, rather than the shortened version used for the same Web server hosted files.

The last point in the paragraph above is worth highlighting. When you store files on a Web server and refer to them using Web pages or links from the same Web server, they will inherit a shortened internal link address such as "*./images/example.jpg*". You should make sure you change these to the full external address e.g., "*www.websitename.cm/imagsexample.jpg*". This is because the feed could be syndicated by other Web sites where the file will no longer be locally stored.

Some search engines index personal home pages faster than other Web pages (typically within 48 hours). Therefore, store your RSS on your iGoogle.com, my.Yahoo.com and my.Msn.com home pages, as well as on your Web site. They will be indexed quickly and be searchable on the main search engine's RSS feeds database.

RSS publishers have categories in which they list RSS feeds. Make it easy on yourself and list your feeds under the most relevant feeds category, rather than being dumped in the "miscellaneous" or "other" group. Sometimes this selection is automated due to your content, XML tags or title.

Similarly, use a template or theme to create your document. Try and select one that lists or aligns the title and text to the left. This is better for SEO, as search engines pick up text more readily from the left-hand side.

When naming your Feed, select a title that starts with "A". This is because many subscribers view their feeds in alphabetical order. This will give yourself the chance to be near the top.

Use a single URL for your feeds. If you have multiple locations for a feed, changing the URL could cause you to lose subscribers. If you have multiple feeds, sign up to a feed management service such as that run by www.feedburner.com. You can point all your feeds there and manage the forwarding or real location details from Feedburner, so that subscribers have a seamless subscription service.

If you are linking to a specific section of a page in your feed, set up a bookmark in the page so that you can use the exact link to the correct section, rather than cause the subscriber to search for the appropriate section themselves. As an example: If you wanted to link to the "Organizations That Can Help" section at http://ultimategamblingsystems.com /Support/responsiblegambling.htm, you could bookmark the appropriate section and use the following to link directly to that section: http://ultimategamblingsystems.com/Support /responsiblegambling.htm#4._Organisations_That_Can_Help. (The # denotes that an in-page link is to follow).

Add a company logo to give the RSS added professionalism. Use the same logo with each RSS you publish to build a corporate brand. Soon, people will recognize your feeds by your logo.

Always check to make sure that your feeds work and are correctly formatted before submitting them to your publisher. Use www.feedvalidator.org to validate your feeds.

All the major search engines offer an *"Add to My..."* button. Make sure you include these in your feed to make it easy for people to subscribe to your feed.

Yahoo! offers the *Yahoo! Browse-by-Topic Directory* as an additional service that will get your blog even more exposure. This service does not guarantee that your RSS will be included, as their editorial staff must check the RSS first. Furthermore, if you are selected, be aware that Yahoo! could change the title and description of your RSS.

Whoever you decide to publish your RSS with, take your time and research their services so that you can compare their competitors and evaluate the benefits and disadvantages. Always submit your RSS to the correct directories, such as:

- Blogs: www.blog-connection.com/submit-blogs.htm
- Podcasts: www.podcasting-tools.com/submit-podcasts.htm
- RSS Feeds:www.rss-specifications.com/rss-submission.htm

Always follow submission guidelines and select categories carefully. After submitting, be the first to subscribe to your own feed, blog or podcast. This is to make sure that everything is working fine and also to to give you information about how your subscribers will experience the subscription. Submitting to your own RSS could also help you improve on formatting and arrangement of future feeds.

Really simple syndication tools (RSS):

- **RSS Specifications**– Comprehensive RSS reference detailing everything you need to know about RSS: www.rss-specifications.com.
- **RSS Tools**–Learn how to use the power of RSS: www.rss-tools.com.

Pod Casting

A podcast is an online audio content syndicated via RSS. Podcasts are great for promoting music, books, talk shows, instructional training materials, storytelling or for other purposes, such as self-guided walking tours.

Because they are syndicated, they can be subscribed to just as blogs and other media content feeds can be subscribed to through RSS.

To get started, you need a microphone, sound recording and sound editing software or equipment. The files need to be MP3 format. Upload them to your Web site, podcast publisher, or file store. Then create a feed, link the MP3 file to the feed, include a description title and bookmarking links, and submit.

The rest is just as advised for feeds, except you promote your podcast at different sites as well as your social networking site. For further information on podcasting, visit:

- A decentralized, categorized directory of links to podcast feeds: www.ipodder.org/directory/4/podcasts
- http://en.wikipedia.org/wiki/Podcasting
- Podcast search engine: www.podscope.com
- Volunteer podcast directory: www.podnovacom

Peer-to-Peer (P-2-P)

Peer-to-peer refers to the collective sharing of Internet bandwidth, computer processing power and storage space across a diverse user base of computers. Participants share files from their computers with other members of the network who can download these files, and in turn, allow others to download their files.

Because P-2-P networks allow people to share files and they are almost wholly unregulated, a lot of copyright infringement activity goes on. People share documents, pictures, video, films, music, entire applications and much more, all for free. You can read more on peer-to-peer at http://en.wikipedia.org/wiki/peer-to-peer.

Today there are many types of peer-to-peer solutions and networks. Some are centralized, others are decentralized and still others are a hybrid of both.

Today, most peer-to-peer services use the bittorrent communication protocol. This protocol allows the sharing of large files without a single provider incurring the entire cost of supply. Instead, everyone who has copy of the same file contributes a small portion of the file to the requester, thus cutting down on the supply overhead (CPU, hard drive, power, bandwidth and costs).

To use the bittorrent protocol, you first need to install a peer-to-peer client that supports bittorrent. First, install a firewall, antivirus software, spyware and AdWare protection softwares on your computer. Visit Microsoft.com, Apple.com or your operating system's manufacturers' Web site for more details.

Next, visit www.bittorrent.com or search for "bittorrent client" on any major search engine for a peer-to-peer client software which supports bittorrent. Once you have installed the client software, simply search for what you want, either with the peer-to-peer client, or by using a search engine. If using a search engine, search for, "bittorrent [the name of the file you are looking for]". For example, "bittorrent holy bible".

This technological phenomenon has, and is still, causing the music and film industry serious concerns and financial losses. However, there is a good point to all this. It is great for those who are looking for something for free, and it also offers another means of promoting your Web site, product or services.

You can do so through advertising on the download pages of the hottest download files. You can find out what the hottest downloads are from the following sites, or search for "best bittorrent Web site".

- http://mybittorrent.com
- www.isohunt.com
- www.mininova.org
- www.thepiratebay.org
- www.torrentz.com

Another popular method is to look for and download one of the hottest "legal" downloads. Place a promotion of your Web site (site name and link address) at the beginning of an audio, video or within an image. Then, add a transparent footer or header on the actual file, if it is an image file or video. Imbed the promotion in such a way so that it cannot be easily removed without greatly affecting the quality of the media file.

You can also produce your own media files and leak them onto the peer-to-peer networks. Your success will be limited using this methodand will depend on the popularity of your media file production.

WARNING: Armies of hackers utilize peer-to-peer networks to promote their efforts. They are often highly talented and will reverse engineer almost any security feature you may employ. Therefore, be careful in using peer-to-peer to promote any copyrighted product. It will not stay secure for long. Organizations constantly seek to sue abusers of their copyright. Unless you are sure you are not in breach of copyright, do not attach your name and Web site to any illegally distributed media file.

Copyright.

Normally, for the best SEO and SMO results, you have to allow your creations to be copied and shared. Creative Commons (a Massachusetts-chartered 501(c)(3) tax-exempt charitable corporation), offers copyrights to assist with this. You can also choose to draft your own, or create a new one by amending another one.

However you choose to copyright your work, be sure you specify that certain portions of your work (i.e., your name or company name and Web site link), must always remain with all transmission(s) for re-use of your material. For more information, contact:

- Creative Commons: http://creativecommons.org
- UK Copyright Office: www.ipo.gov.uk/copy.htm
- US Copyright Office: www.copyright.gov

Search Engine Optimization

Chapter 4

Driving Sales Traffic

Internet Sales

According to The Center for Economics and Business Research (www.cebr.com), online shoppers in the UK are expected to spend £162 billion ($336 billion), per year on products via the Internet by 2020. Their prediction on British e-commerce sales for 2008 is £40 billion or ($82 billion).

Adding to these figures is eMarketer (www.emarketer .com), predicting that online advertisers will pay $42 billion on Internet advertising by 2011, and they expect $21.4 billion to be spent by the end of 2008.

The future promises more online sales according to all e-commerce research. How are you going to benefit from this? In this chapter we will look closely at the various SEO methods available to you for increasing your Internet sales. We will look at six main categories of Internet marketing:

- Affiliation
- Auction
- Banner
- E-Mail
- Free & Low Cost Advertisement
- Paid Inclusion

Free and Low Cost Advertising

Free advertising deals with sources of advertising that costs you nothing. One of these is on your own Web site. You would be surprised at how many people miss the opportunity to promote other sections of their Web site, other products and services or even associated Web sites from their Web site.

Whether your Web site sells products or services, you should use every opportunity to market them throughout your site. As we have covered already, the links to other sections of your Web site will help your site's page rank and help to retain visitors within your site. Don't just depend on your navigation links to take your visitors to other sections of your Web site, give them an incentive to go there with linked text within the content, linked images or linked ads.

Aside from your own Web site, there are a host of other sources that offer the opportunity of advertising for free. Here is a list of some of them:

1) Ad Pages—Web pages that allow free advertisement placement. Search for "ad sites" or "FFA sites".
   Pros: It is free.
   Cons: Your advertisement only lasts a few days/hours or minutes, due to over subscription.

2) Events Pages—Advertise your launches, openings, day outs, charity drives, shows, etc.
   Pros: It is free with localized, targeted visitors.
   Cons: It is short term, you need an event to promote, only reaches a small local audience.

3) Pixel Pages—Advertise by placing a single pixel or more linked to your Web site. Search for "pixel site".
   Pros: It is free.
   Cons: Free pixel sites can attract junk sites.

4) Search Engine Home Pages—geocities.yahoo.com, igoogle.com, live.com, my.yahoo.com, are some examples of these.
   Pros: It is free and indexed quickly. Some are more likely to be included in SERPs.
   Cons: Need to promote them also and you don't control the domain. Limited functionality sites. Can be slow.

5) Web Space—Providers of free Web space, similar to search engine home pages but not provided by search engines *See;* www.freebielist.com/webspace.htm.
   Pros: Free space from which to host sites.
   Cons: Sites will need promotion and you do not control the domain. Limited functionality sites. Can be slow.

6) Limited Time Free & Paid Inclusion—PPC and CPI sites that allow a limited, free trial service. *See;* www.grudd .com/html/grudd_com_advertising.html
   Pros: Get pay-per-click and cost-per-impression free.
   Cons: Limited use. Needs constant changing.

7) Banner Advertising—Normally you display one or two banner ads to earn your banner being displayed once. *See;* www.allaboutlinks.net/link-exchange.aspx, and www.no1 bannerexchange.com.
   Pros: Get free banner ads.
   Cons: Need to install widget or add code to your site.

8) Button Advertising—Small banners ads (buttons), as small as 88 x 31 pixels. *See;* www.hotcandle.com.
   Pros: Same as banner advertising; free, small and less disruptive to the aesthetics of your Web site.
   Cons: Need to install widget or add code to your site.

9) BizAds Advertising—Placing free advertisements on business classified pages. *See;* www.cweb.net, and www.loot.com.
   Pros: It is free, simple and has many sources offering the service.
   Cons: If using too many, can get unmanageable and most are limited to text only. Although Web-link allowed, (premium members can have pictures and other features), but it has strong competition.

10) Business Directories—Free listing in business "yellow pages" type of directory *See;* www.uksmallbusiness directory.co.uk, http://dir.yahoo.com, http://specials.msn .com, www.google.com/Top/Business and www.the-business-list.com.
    Pros: It is free and puts your business where it can be found by directory users.
    Cons: You will often be limited to one entry only at most directories. The classifications can be restrictive.

11) Classifieds—Free classified advertisements. *See* www.usfreeads.com, http://uk.freeads.net, www.loot.com and www.adtrader.co.uk.
    Pros: It is free and ad is easy to place.
    Cons: High competition and many providers make it hard to manage.

12) E-mail Advertising—Use the power of e-mail to promote your business. We will cover this in more detail on page 115.

13) FFA & Links Pages—Free for all pages and anyone can post their Web site address. Because anyone can post to them however, they can fill up quickly and thus knock your address off the page. This can take days, hours or in some cases minutes, depending on the rate that addresses are being added. If you insist on trying it, *See*; www.ffanet.com or http://blastomatic.com.
Pros: It is free, easy to use and offers many choices.
Cons: Rubbish mainly, requires constant re-submission and adds little to no SEO value. This site will also send you junk mail and spam for years.

14) Traffic Exchanges—This service matches your surfing of selected Web sites (with a time interval, normally between 10 and 20 seconds), with directed traffic to your Web site. *See* http://del.icio.us, and also see Appendix 7, pg. 208 for a complete list of traffic exchange sites.
Pros: It is free with immediate traffic you can control.
Cons: Waste of time just clicking away. Also, visitors tend to do what you might do, they wait until the time is up and click away from your site in order to earn their traffic.

15) Advertising Groups—Group which allows business and Web site advertising. Only stipulation with some of them is that the advertisements must be relevant to the group. *See* http://iam.homewithgod.com/glimpsesofgod/addurlink2.html, http://small-budget-advertising.com/free_advertising_groups.htm.
Pros: It is free with a highly targeted, relevant audience.
Cons: High competition. Many restrict use of HTML, apart from a Web link in your signature.

16) Bulletin Boards—We have discussed bulletin boards in the previous chapter. The bulletin boards that are free to join are the most cost effective to use for promoting and advertising your business. You can advertise through the

media you upload, through the forums and the news feeds. *See* Bulletin Boards on page 61.
Pros: Can be free.
Cons: Offeres limited choice and content compared to the Internet.

17) Web Pages—We have already covered FFA's, however, other Web sites may also offer you a chance of advertising through comments, reviews, uploads, submissions, link exchanges and back-linking for free.

Visit your competitor's Web sites and the sites of those not directly in competition with you, but that are attracting traffic which could benefit from the information, products or services your Web site offers.

Wherever you are permitted to post a review or comment, do so, especially if the site is relevant to your Web site's content and it allows inclusion of Web links.

We have already discussed back-links in the section on Link Boosting, (page 30), and how you can contact Web site owners to inquire if they would link to your site. If they agree to do so for free, you would have gained a back-link, potential traffic and possible page rank increase.
Pros: Can be free.
Cons: Can be time consuming and difficult to manage.

18) Advertising Forums—Forums which allow advertisers to post ads. They are similar to classifieds, but they support threads. Others can post in your thread, thus extending the thread. You do not control the thread. It is generally best to find a hot topic and regularly add your comments and ads into it, as opposed to starting a new one that you own. For more information, visit the following sites:

- http://freeads.biztop.com
- http://postadsfree.forumwise.com
- http://postfreeads.free-forums.org
- www.freeadsforum.com
- www.freeadvertisingboard.com

- www.postfreeadsforum.com
- www.postyouradforfree.com

Pros: It is free and allows multiple advertisement posts within the forum, allows you to cater the advertisement to the audience and even start a discussion of how the advertisement can be improved.

Cons: Competition and spam. As the thread grows your advertisement sinks into obscurity requiring you to regularly resubmit a variation of the advertisement. It can have strict rules so read the rules of use carefully and follow them.

19) Blogs—Journal type post using text with supporting links and HTML, which can be syndicated. *See page* 65.

20) Vlogs—Post using moving images, text with supporting links and HTML, which can be syndicated. *See page* 70.

21) Photo-blogs—Diary post using images, text with supporting links and HTML, which can be syndicated. *See page* 68.

22) Podcasts—Type of diary using MP3 files with supporting links and HTML. *See page* 88.

Banner Advertising

Banner advertisements are found on Web pages, blogs, forums and groups, etc., in the form of a linked banner image. The image can be animated or a static (non-moving) picture. Banner sizes vary from "buttons" (80 x 15 pixels) to half page "skyscrapers" (300 x 600 pixels). Their size is measured in pixel width x height.

Creation of effective banner advertisements is considered by some as an art form. However, there are steps that can greatly improve the effectiveness of your banner ads. The following are a few of the most important steps to take for greatest success:

1) Find out what your competition is doing and what seems to be working the best for them. No need to reinvent the wheel. Get a cross section of your competitions' banner

ads and note what is good about each. Isolate the things you like, note it down and keep the points in mind as you work on your banner advertisement. You may not like any of your competitors' banner ads. Try not to let your personal preferences get in the way of selecting an effective solution. Remember, you are looking for an advertisement that gets results; click-through and traffic.

2) Decide on the size and orientation of your banner. The size will dictate to a large extent what you can include with the banner. Normally the place to be displayed will restrict your choice of sizes, however if you have a choice and the cost is the same, always opt for a larger banner to be placed at the top of the page.

3) Keep the design simple. Research shows that two or three contrasting colors get more click-throughs than a banner with all the colors of the rainbow. Remember, people have only a few seconds to understand what your advertisement is saying and to remember it. Therefore, keep the details so simple that the banner can be understood at a glance. You also want to make it stand out enough to immediately catch the visitor's attention. This will require you to have different banner designs for different Web sites. In each Web site's case, the contrasting colors must change to complement the background colors of the Web page.

4) If you are going to use words, and I highly advise you to do so, make sure you simplify the slogan or message as much as possible. You want to have the text or sentence short enough to maximize its font size, and you want the viewer to be able to discern what is written with just a glance. Use keywords that are heavily used on the page in which you are planning on displaying the banner advert.

5) Use a little animation. The movement helps attract attention to the banner. However, don't overdo animation. Try and keep animation under five seconds.

6) Try and keep the file size below 50 kilobytes (KB). You should be able to achieve this if you limit the color palette

and animation sequence length. If your banner advert is aimed at attracting users with powerful PCs and broadband connections, you may be a little more lenient on the banner file size. However, if not, then try to limit the banner size to a minimum. It is possible to build a great banner from 14KB in size.

7) Make sure your landing page seals the sale when visitors click-through. This is will require exceptional copywriting. You may need to seek the help of a professional copywriter to ensure that the landing page is effective at converting click-through visitors into customers. Try www.ifreelance.com, where you can post your project and let copywriters bid to obtain your business, or search for a professional/freelance copywriter through www .freelanceuk.com/copywriters. Whatever you do, never underestimate the power of a well written and edited sales page. It can hold the key to success or failure for your banner advertisement campaign.

8) Obtain, or insist on tracking the click-throughs and conversion rates, from your banner advertisement campaign. Being able to know the type of traffic you are receiving, its origin, how it reacted to your landing page and how many conversions-to-sales you received is vital to fine-tuning your advertisement. Choose the right place to display your banner ads.

9) Answers to these questions will lead you closer to discovering the faults or opportunities for improvement within your advertisement campaign. Using your traffic statistic, identify the following:

   a. Are you targeting the right audience?
   b. Is the landing page appropriate for the audience?
   c. Is your product too cheap or too expensive?
   d. How are click-through visitors exiting your landing page?

10) Make sure you have an effective landing page. *See page* 110 for more details on creating one.

11) Finally, don't stop learning to write better copy. Visit the sites www.freelanceuk.com/copywriters or visit www .amazon.com for books on copywriting and try (Bly, 1990) *The Copywriter's Handbook, Third Edition: A Step-By-Step Guide To Writing Copy That Sells* by Robert W. Bly, or (Gabay, 2007) *Gabay's Copywriters' Compendium-*revised edition in paperback: *The Definitive Professional Writers Guide* by Jonathan Gabay.

An alternative to creating your own banner advertisement campaign is to have one professionally created for you. There are many companies that will gladly take your money and produce a banner, and even arrange the distribution of the banner, on relevant Web sites at a cost. One of the largest pay-per-click and cost-per-impressions service providers is Google AdWords. Normally, this cost is relative to your PPC or CPI cost thresholds. Therefore, you can pay to be included on banner space at participating Web sites. Let us take a closer look at paid inclusion programs.

Paid Inclusion

Getting listed on some search engines can literally take months. This is because the schedule for the crawler is so busy that if you do not pay a premium to be fast tracked, your site will not be considered for a long time. To speed up the process, some search engines (*not* Google or Ask.com), allow Web masters to pay to have their Webs listed or crawled faster and more frequently, typically once a week.

It is important to understand that paid inclusion promises only to index you quicker and more regularly; not to improve your page rank. However, in many cases if you are running an SEO campaign, getting listed quickly will go some way towards your campaign getting to work earlier to improve your page rank.

It normally costs a fixed annual price and the more Web addresses you submit at the same time, the more the cost of paid inclusion decreases. Yahoo! Search Marketing is the main paid inclusion provider. They offer *Search Submit* and *Search Submit Pro*. Find out more from:

- http://searchmarketing.yahoo.com/srchsb.
- http://searchmarketing.yahoo.com/srchsb/ssb.php
- http://searchmarketing.yahoo.com/srchsb/ssp.php

Yahoo! Search Marketing also offers some specialist services, namely, Product Submit at (http://searchmarketing. yahoo.com/shopsb) and Travel Submit at (http://search marketing.yahoo.com/trvlsb). These two services place ads of your products and travel deals, respectfully, at prominent positions on SERPs, at an extra cost.

Local businesses may also be interested in Yahoo! Search Marketing's local listing service. It offers guaranteed prominent placement of your Web site listing in http://local.yahoo.com. *See* http://searchmarketing.yahoo.com /local, for more information.

Paid Directory Review

Paid directory review is a paid inclusion for directories. Normally when you submit your Web site to a directory for review, and prior to an inclusion decision, the time until review can take months. (And when directories operate a paid directory program, you have to wonder if the delay for unpaid reviews is intentional). A paid directory review allows you to shortcut this process for a fee. Normally for adult site reviews, the charge is doubled.

For Yahoo! Directories the fee is currently $299 ($600 for adult sites), just for the review. If your site is not accepted into the directory, you will not be refunded your fee. If your site is accepted to be listed in the directory, you will be charged a further $299 ($600 for adult sites), per annum to maintain the listing. If you do not pay, you are not listed. *See* http://dir.yahoo.com for further details.

There is good news however, www.dmoz.org which is a free submission directory, supplies directory listings to AOL Search, AltaVista, HotBot, Google, Lycos and more, and you can therefore get listed in these sites for free. Their directories are maintained by, and new submissions are reviewed by, a huge volunteer network of people.

Even if you are listed on Yahoo!, I advise that you also submit your site to www.dmoz.org. As with all directories, their submission rules are strict and you could easily get rejected if you try to submit into the wrong subdirectory. It is highly recommended that you read their instructions carefully.

They only allow one listing per site and reject any attempts to submit the same content under another name. They are thorough and will pick up on any attempts at cheating the directory review process.

What I can suggest however, is that if you have a broad range of content on your site, that you create smaller sites to host just the subsets of your main, big site. Submit these content subset sites to the directory separately. You will be able to get more of your content in the relevant sections of the directory using this method.

Paid Links

The practice of purchasing links from higher page ranked sites does two things. Firstly, it boosts your page rank instantly; secondly it increases the chances of you being *blacklisted* by a search engine. This is especially true if you sell page links. The largest search engine in the world, Google, has taken a strong stance against this practice.

Google recognizes that not all paid links are in violation of their guidelines, also they recognize that links are bought and sold frequently for advertising purposes. They draw the line, however, where it is done to manipulate search engine rank. Google advises the use of either:

- Adding a rel="nofollow" attribute to the <a> tag.
- Redirecting the links to an intermediate page that is blocked from search engines with a robots.txt file.

It's hard to tell how many paid link sellers actually follow Googles guidelines, however, I suspect there are few. After all, most people who buy paid links, do so specifically to manipulate their search rank. Similarly, sellers of page rank do so to further capitalize on their higher page ranks.

I will leave the decision whether you should participate in this crime against the major search engines between you and your conscience.

> **WARNING:** Buying paid links simply to fool the search engines is frowned upon by the major search engines. If caught, you stand a chance of having the benefits removed or worse; being dropped in page rank even further than you previously were without the paid links.

That said, for all of you honest folks out there who use paid links for legitimate advertising purposes, here are a few links to some helpful sites:

W3C: www.w3.org/Consortium/sup

What value contribution is required to be listed here?
- Premier Supporters have made a contribution of ≥ 10000 USD (or equivalent in another currency).
- Major Supporters have made a contribution of 1000 - 9999 USD (or equivalent in another currency).
- Contributing Supporters have made a contribution of 100 - 999 USD (or equivalent in another currency).

Linkadage
www.linkadage.com/auction:
As a medium for selling and buying links; they offer link buying directly from sellers, through auction, brokerage and links exchanging. It also has a tool for analyzing links' PR data and metrics of links against keywords.

Linksnow
www.linksnow.com: Trades and promotes links with other members.

The best way to get your "advertising" paid links, is secretly. This is because as soon as the SEO crowd catches a whiff that a high rank site is prepared, and in fact engaged in, selling paid links, they all come knocking at the door; some offering more money for a paid link, while others take actions to demote the high rank.

Contact the owners of high PR sites covertly, negotiate yourself a deal and keep it a secret for as long as it will naturally last, which is not long on the World Wide Web; but at least it will give you a head start on the competition.

Paid Placement: Pay-Per-Click (PPC)

If you have the budget and want the ultimate in SEO success techniques, you can turn to PPC. Whether you are selling a product, service or simply want more traffic to your site, blog or feeds, PPC can ensure success. PPC allows you to enter into an auction where you can specify your bid limits, or set a fixed price (that you are prepared to pay), for a paid listing for searches of specific keywords and keyword phrases.

The paid listings are then sorted according to the highest bidder first. If you fall within the top listed, your advertisement will be displayed. The more you are prepared to pay-per-click, the higher placed in the list you will become. The limits are therefore only set by your budget.

Of course everyone would love to be at the top. However, what matters once you are in the top listings displayed is that your advertisement takes over, and does the rest for you. Will it attract the viewer's attention and attract a click-through, or not?

Your advertisement is the key to PPC success. It must grab attention and cause visitors to click on the linked advertisement. Once they click on the advertisement your landing page takes over. It must lead the visitor into buying your product or service. Let us analyze these three steps in more detail:

1) Bid high enough to be listed.
2) Have a click magnet of an advertisement.
3) Have a successful sales driven landing page that will generate sales.

Now we will analyze these key points, one by one:

Bidding Techniques for PPC

Most people believe by using PPC that you have to get to the top. That is not true. Listings that are ranked second, third or fourth are still on the first page and have a high chance of attracting the visitor, if the listings are captivating.

With that in mind, aim to be on the first page every time or if not, then aim to be at the top or bottom of the second page. The bottom of the page is normally where the navigation links to subsequent pages are found. The visitor is more likely to see your catchy advertisement at the bottom of the page than in the middle.

By aiming your advertisement at the bottom of the page or the top of the second page, you will pay far less per click than aiming for pole position.

1) Ad Groups

With PPC as we have already mentioned, you bid on keywords and keyword phrases. You can select the keywords that are most specific to your landing page and start by bidding the lowest for them. If your keyword selection is poor, you may end up having to pay more per click, than if your landing page's relevancy was perfectly matching your keyword group for the PPC advertisement.

To make sure you pay the least for keywords and keyword phrases, list all the most relevant and popular keywords for your landing product and service, separate them into smaller, highly relevant groups centered around one or two keywords or keyword phrases.

You can set up many of these small keyword relevant groups. Each paying a fraction of how much you would have to pay for all of them in a single PPC advertisement group.

Furthermore, make sure your advertisement contains these keywords and that your landing page is full of them. By having the keywords in the advertisement text spread across many smaller ad groups and all assigned to relevant key worded ads, you will drive highly relevant traffic to the landing page.

Traffic will cost you less per click than if your keyword group was spread across less relevant, or a broader range of keywords and keyword phrases.

2) Conversion Rate

How many clicks is your advertisement converting into sales? If your advertisement is being clicked on like crazy but you are converting less than 10% of those clicks into sales, it could highlight a problem with your landing page, or the type of traffic you are attracting with your keyword group.

If you are attracting a lot of traffic from people who want everything for free, such as students and researchers, their clicks will not convert into sales. Make sure your advertisement is not trying to be clever by driving "just any" traffic to your landing page, in the hope of getting more sales. Quality traffic will bring more sales than quantity traffic.

Look at your stats for conversion rates, analyze your advertisement copy and revisit and tweak your landing page. It is better if you get one hundred clicks a day and convert half of them into sales, rather than getting a thousand clicks a day and only converting five percent. The latter will cost you more in PPC fees and make lose you money against the former.

3) Providers

- Ask Sponsored Listings: http://sponsoredlistings.ask.com
- Enhance Interactive: www.enhance.com
- ePilot Advertising Network: www.epilot.com
- Google AdWords: https://adwords.google.com
- Kanoodle: www.kanoodle.com
- LookSmart LookListings: https://adcenter.looksmart.com
- Mirago: www.mirago.com
- Miva: www.miva.com
- Search 123: http://search123.com
- Yahoo! Search Marketing: http://searchmarketing.yahoo.com

Each of the PPC programs listed offers extensive online support and FAQs, with some also offering offline telephone support. Contact them and find out how they can help you.

The Sales Ad

As Google AdWords is the largest, most influential PPC program, we shall next analyze what you should and should not do with your Google AdWords ads. The same advice in most cases applies to all other PPC programs.

Don't use a long list of unpopular or irrelevant keywords. Instead, work with a shorter list of highly targeted, relevant and popular keywords that are featured heavily on your landing page. Use these keywords to create your advertisement wording.

In your advertisement, identify unique points about your product or service. For instance, if your product is uniquely colored green, include that in your keywords. "Green wedding dress" is much better than "wedding dress".

Use a specially created landing page. It doesn't have to be on a separate domain to your Web site, although it must be specific to your advertisement. The keywords you selected must be heavily featured in the landing page. Link this landing page to your advertisement.

As already mentioned, use multiple, specific, targeted and relevant advertisement groups with multiple advertisement campaigns. Split your keywords and keyword phrases into unique groups and apply multiple advertisement groups to your multiple Google AdWords advertisements.

Select the best times and locations in which you wish your advertisement to run. Don't send it everywhere at just anytime. Remember different demographics will bring different traffic and different conversion rates.

All PPC and Web advertising programs offer tools for tracking your ads. They give you key statistics so that you evaluate the effectiveness of your advertisement campaign. Track these stats and monitor them. Learn to read and combine them to create more useful statistics for your particular purpose. Match them to your sales results to determine conversion rates.

Make sure you set your budget. Most PPC programs allow you to set the daily spending and cost-per-click expenditures. You can usually set your monthly budget limit; use these budgeting tools to your advantage. Restrict your spending before enabling the advertisement campaign.

Landing Page

With every Internet advertisement campaign, you need to make sure the page that visitors land on, after they click the advertisement, is sales driven and effective at converting "clickers" or visitors, into buyers. Keep monitoring and tweaking your advertisement. Observe the following points for writing and designing your landing page:

- Understand the needs of your targeted audience. What are their fears, what do they want, what are their tolerances, what do they hate?
- Select a simple design for your landing page. A simple template looks more professional than a cluttered page.
- Have more than one column. Separate your page into four columns; merge the three on the far left so that you have one wide column and a thin one.
- Stay focused on the purpose of the text- getting a sale. Everything you write must support that goal.
- Write a short, catchy headline and follow with a lead paragraph that will relate to the target audience immediately. Don't make the lead too long because most people will not read that far.
- To add credibility; show your photo, company name, address, phone number and offer a short biography. Build on your credibility with testimonials and images of people who have successfully used the product or service.
- Offer a guarantee and mention it several times.
- Experiment with different prices to discover the price that customers are willing to pay. You can get this statistic from running tests at different prices. Start at the highest

first and work your way down until you discover which price was most successful.

- Think of other products or services you can market to your customers after the sale. Imagine what type of people they are and what their other needs might be. It is easier to sell to a target audience you have had past success with, than to totally new demographics.

Visit the following links for further help on creating effective landing pages:

- http://services.google.com/websiteoptimizer
- www.omniture.com
- www.widemile.com

Affiliate Networks and Affiliation

If you are interested in being affiliated with any manufacturer or service provider, first check their Web site for an "*affiliate program*", and if they don't offer affiliation directly, they may offer it through an affiliate program such as Trade Doubler.

The large affiliate programs offer a vast range of payment options, earning options and clients. For instance, most insurance companies use affiliate marketing through one of these programs, or an agent who then publishes their services via an affiliate program.

Become an affiliate by adding products and services to your Web site. The process varies from one affiliate program to the other. The program's site will have help and support details on exactly how to achieve this. The following are some great affiliation sites:

- Amazon: http://affiliateprogram.amazon.com/gp/associates/join
- Apple iTunes: www.apple.com/itunes/affiliates
- Sony: www.sonystyle.com
- Thomas Cook: www.thomascook.com/content/help/help-lp/affiliates.asp
- XL: www.xl.com/About_Us/Affiliates.asp

Affiliate Programs

- https://chitika.com
- www.affiliatecommission.us
- www.affiliatefuel.com
- www.affiliatefuture.co.uk
- www.affiliatemarketing.co.uk
- www.affiliatewindow.com
- www.amwso.com
- www.cj.com
- www.clickbank.com
- www.clickxchange.com
- www.clixgalore.com
- www.linkshare.com
- www.microsoftaffiliates.net
- www.partnercentric.com
- www.performics.com
- www.shareasale.com
- www.shareresults.com
- www.tradedoubler.com
- www.valuecommerce.ne.jp
- www.westernunion.com/info/aboutUsAffiliate.asp
- www.widgetbucks.com

eBay

eBay is an online auction Web site. It is an Internet success phenomenon. There are over fifteen million members helping eBay turn over $60 billion in sales per annum. Furthermore, eBay represents an incredible marketing tool. How can you make money from this incredible SEO tool? Here is what you need to know:

eBay allows sellers and buyers to trade through an auction system; whereby sellers place their products or services up for auction or for sale at a fixed price. Buyers bid on the auctioned goods or outright purchase the goods, that are for sale. Today, almost anything you can imagine is available in some form on eBay.

The Web site, www.ebay.com and its other sites carry a lot of traffic. A high proportion of the traffic is looking to spend money, since they are generally looking to buy something.

You can set up an eBay account and start your own auctions; however, there is more SEO benefit to using the eBay tool in other ways. One of these is to set up an eBay shop. The process to do this is as follows:

1. Open an account at www.paypal.com.
2. Open an account at https://scgi.ebay.com.
3. Meet the qualification criteria:
   a) Have an eBay seller's account with your credit card placed on file.
   b) Have a feedback score of 20 or higher, be ID verified or have a PayPal account in good standing.

If you meet these requirements, you can open an eBay store. *See* (http://cgi6.ebay.com/ws/eBayISAPI.dll?Store frontLogin).

eBay offers extensive help on using their system and setting up your store. Visit the eBay specialty site's help at (http://pages.ebay.com/help /specialtysites), for more details.

Once you open your store, you can learn how to begin listing with the Store Inventory format. There are some similarities with what we have covered already in the previous chapters. These are as follows:

- Store Naming and URL – the name you give your store will also be appended to the eBay.com URL, to give you a direct URL to your shop. Therefore, name your store with a name that is:
  a) Descriptive of what you will be selling.
  b) Uses popular, relevant keywords.
  c) Short, no more than three words long.
- Store Description – describe your store with popular, relevant keywords that perfectly describe the contents of the shop. Use a store that aligns your description text to the left.

Search Engine Optimization

- Custom Pages – there are different levels of eBay subscription. With each subscription level comes different options for custom pages. Normally the following is true:
  a) The more you pay, the more custom Web pages you are allowed in your shop. However many custom pages you get, utilize them all.
  b) Use them to give credibility to your shop.
  c) Keep them sales focused.
  d) Link to each one from each page.
- Custom Categories – you get virtual shelves in your shop.
  a) You can use up to 300 per shop.
  b) Name them with relevant, popular keywords which describe exactly what they will contain.
  c) Do not use generic terms.
  d) Try and keep the custom names as specific, simple and short as possible.
- Listing Headers – at the top of your store you will have a listing header.
  a) Always include your store name, a link to your store's home page and your store's colors.
  b) You can add to this:

    - Store logo.
    - Search box enabling buyers to search your store.
    - A link that enables buyers to add you to their favorite sellers list.
    - A link that enables buyers to sign up for your e-mail marketing newsletters.
    - Links to your custom categories, custom pages and an 'About Me' page (up to a maximum of 5 links).

  c) Use as many of the extra header add-ons as possible, especially links to your other shop pages.

- Search Engine Keywords – assign keywords to your shop. eBay uses these to create Page titles and META tags for your products and pages. Make sure you fill these in with highly relevant keywords. eBay allows primary and secondary keywords. The primary should be the most relevant and popular. The secondary should be related and derivatives of the primary i.e., if "diamond" is the primary keyword, "diamond ring, diamond watch, colored diamond, diamonds," etc., could be the secondary.

Next, upload your products and their details.

If you purchased a Pro Store, you will have a few more SEO options to tweak. *See* http://pages.ebay.com/education /SEO-ProStores for details on doing this.

Another way is to affiliate your eBay shop; allowing others to sell your products on eBay for the same price as your shop, but you pay these affiliates a commission on each sale. You will find a list of eBay's dos and don'ts at http://pages.ebay.com/education/SEO-best-practices. Follow their recommendations carefully.

eBay recommends the following resources to help you with SEO issues. See the link at eBay University for comprehensive eBay schooling, from the basics to beyond. Find them at:

SEO Chat	Marketleap	eBay University
www.seochat. com	www.marketleap.com/defau lt.htm	http://pages.ebay.com/u niversity

Table 6: Pro-Store SEO eBay Help/Options

E-mail and Safelist Advertising

Market to the e-mail opt-in addresses of subscribers to your Web site. You can also join an e-mail autoresponder exchange whereby you receive an advertisement by e-mail, every time you send an ad to the autoresponder. Your e-mail advertisement will be pooled and sent to people in the network as you earn credits from e-mailing to the autoresponder. Alternatively, you can also join an e-mail marketing site as a free member and get a limited e-mail marketing service.

Pros: It is free and it reaches more people via e-mail.
Cons: These can often be poor e-mail lists, they can generate spam complaints and frequently the free service is a front to force you to upgrade to a premium service.

Search Engine Optimization

- www.cdconline.com/bizlist/index.html
- www.sendfree.com
- www.submitexpress.com/opt-in-e-mails.html
- http://mailyourad.com

WARNING: E-mail marketing is prone to spam risks. If you are caught spamming, you could get banned by your ISP or by your Web site hosting provider. Always make sure you are using safe lists, or opt-in e-mail addresses. One of the only ways to be 100% sure, is to use your own opt-in e-mail addresses generated from your Web site.

Chapter 5

Monitoring & Fine-Tuning

Monitoring

Now you know many ways of optimizing and promoting your Web site for search engines. You may even have initiated some of the techniques, tips or strategies discussed. How do you know the effectiveness of all your hard work? This is where monitoring comes in. Monitoring the traffic, visitor behavior and calculating effectiveness of SEO campaigns is what this section covers.

Know When You Are Up

First thing is first: You need to know when your Web site is down or unavailable to visitors. After all, what is the use of a great SEO campaign when people can't access your Web site?

Most domain and Web site hosting services offer an e-mail or text messaging service that informs you when your Web site is down. Do not depend soley on the service, however. If something happens that affects the entire functionality of the hosting service provider, they may not be able to send text messages or e-mails. Their entire system could be down. This is the main reason why you need an external monitoring service.

The following are links to Web site monitoring and server downtime alert service providers. Visit one of these sites or search for "web site monitoring" on any of the top search engines:

- http://host-tracker.com
- http://siteimprove.co.uk
- www.alertsite.com
- www.dotcom-monitor.com
- www.is-your-website-up.co.uk
- www.serviceuptime.com
- www.websitepulse.com

You can opt for an text message (SMS) alert to your mobile phone or to your e-mail address when your site is down. The SMS services usually cost more than the e-mail alerts. However, depending on the critical nature of your Web site, you may want to opt for SMS so that you will be informed instantly, the moment your Web site goes down.

If you host your site on a server that you control, you can also choose other services; such as server monitoring and alerting, application and e-mail system monitoring, with round trip checks (end to end e-mail transmission and reception checks and more).

Knowing your Web site and server applications are functioning satisfactorily is the first step in a multi-faceted approach to Web site monitoring. Next, we will look at how to monitor who is visiting to your Web site, where they came from, how they left your site and if they are converted to a potential, or actual customer. You can know these vital elements using monitoring tools.

Monitoring Tools

If a visitor comes to your Web page or Web site and buys a service or product, you have successfully converted them to a customer. If they don't buy anything, but they give their contact information and opt-in to receive product, service or other marketing information, you have converted them into a potential future customer.

Visitors that arrive and depart your Web site without imparting any contact details or buying anything (bounce rate) could spell a potential fault in your SEO and marketing. Perhaps they were misdirected to your site and upon arriving found that it did not contain what they were expecting.

The bounce rate could also point to the fact that you are marketing to the wrong target audience. In the case of no sales, perhaps the target market is not looking to buy anything; such as researchers, students, robots, etc. We will look at how you deal with this issue later in Fine-Tuning; *See page* 132.

Let us next look at the tools we will be using for monitoring Web site traffic and Web site statistics.

Google Webmaster Central

Google offers many free tools for Web masters to monitor, fine-tune and capitalize on their Web sites (www.google.com/webmasters). You may already be aware of AdWords, and site submission. These are not all that Google offers you for improving your Web site traffic and profitability. We will take a closer look at some of the other tools such as Analytics and Web site Optimizer in the next section. For now let's take a closer look at Google Webmaster Tools (www.google. com/webmasters/tools).

Google Webmaster Tools

Google Webmaster Tools is a collection of Web site monitoring, and Googlebot assisting tools that can help you improve how Google sees and indexes your Web site. To access these tools, you need a Google account. Once you log in you will see the Google Webmaster Tools Dashboard; it hosts the Sitemaps Tool we previously looked at.

Add your Web site to the Dashboard with the 'Add Site' button. If you have multiple sites, you can add them all, and use the Webmaster Tools to analyze information from all of them in a user-friendly format.

Next, you will be prompted to verify your Web site. This is a security precaution that demonstrates to Google that you are the owner, or at least you have administrative rights, and can access your Web site files and server.

There are two methods of verification: upload an HTML file with a name generated by Google, or add a Verify META tag, with a Google generated security code, to your Web site's index page.

You can choose not to verify your Web site. However, you will only be allowed to see basic information about your unverified Web site and uploaded sitemaps. You can also view detailed information about the Sitemaps you submit, even if you have not verified your Web site.

The verify META tag will resemble something like this:

```
<meta name="verify-v1" content="S84UKsaTOP7lkS q+
OOh6kNfQsxosT0bCT02N9+9X7w0=" />
```

Once verified, you are ready to use the Google Webmaster Tools to monitor and analyze your Web site information. We shall next look closer at what these tools enable you to do.

Web Crawl

The Googlebot that crawls your Web site to help gather information for the Google index can sometimes have problems with some pages or links. To make sure that the Googlebot was able to crawl your Web site without any problems, use the Web Crawl Tool offered by Google.

This tool helps you see what HTTP errors were encountered by the Googlebot and what links in the Google index the Googlebot was unable to find on your Web site. These dead links would cause your Web server to display a "404 Not found" error message. If you find any dead links, unreachable links or URLs that took too long to resolve, thus causing the Googlebot to give up looking, you can resolve them and avoid further loss of service to visitors.

You can also see what links the robots.txt or robots META tag is restricting the Googlebot from indexing. If there are any links you no longer wish restricted, or if a link is being restricted by accident, you can go to your robots.txt file or the Robots META tags on your Web page and correct the discrepancy.

If your Web site is written in CHTML or WML (these are mobile device Web page formats), you can also check their crawl details. Use the Mobile crawl link on the left-hand side of the Google Webmaster Tools window.

Content Analysis

This tool warns you about content that will reduce your Web page's rank with Google. These are generally issues with Title tags, duplicate, too short or too long META Description tags, and use of non-indexable data, such as flash, video and images.

If the Content Analysis flags any content problems with your Web site, I advise you to correct them immediately to avoid affecting your page rank any further.

Statistics

Google Webmaster Tools offer an array of Web site statistics. These include the following:

- *Top Search Queries* – shows you the top searches and top clicked queries. You can access the data for the past week or the previous six months. You can also select to view data from a variety of Google locations, or view all locations. The search queries also shows you the position you ranked for the search query. Once you can see what search queries are most popularly used to reach your Web site, you can better fine-tune your SEO, thus improving them.

- *What Googlebot Sees* – this statistic shows you how your site is viewed by the Googlebot. It highlights keyword phrases in the internal and external links on your site, and keywords within your Web site's content. This allows you to see what keywords you need to focus on to better align with the external link keywords. Finally, this statistics page also displays the distribution of content type (i.e., text/html, text/xml, application/pdf and text/plain) on your Web site. You can also see statistics for text encodings (i.e., US-ASCII, UTF-8, ISO-8859, etc.) and their distribution throughout your Web site. If the majority of your Web site is in an encoding that is not common to the majority of your visitors, you should change it. Normally UTF-8 is a safe bet.

- *Crawl Stats* – this is a statistic representing the sum of your Web site Google Page Rank. These are illustrated graphically; by distribution bars representing high, medium, low, or not yet assigned. This is useful for quickly seeing where your Page Rank lies. I suggest your goal should always be to move your ranking up to the next level, (unless you are already at high). This statistic refers to Google.com only.

- *Index Stats* – Google offers advanced search functionality via their search engine, allowing people to use 'Site:', 'Link:', 'Cache:', 'Info:' and 'Related:' queries to find specific details about your Web site. This statistic shows you the links to these advanced searches. Of importance are 'Link:', 'Cache', and 'Info:'. Use 'Link:' to see what other Web pages link to your Web site's pages. Use 'Cache:' to see what cached pages Google holds of your site. If the cached pages are older than the current live version, you may want to decrease the duration between Googlebot visits. Finally, 'Info:' will show you what people see when your Web site is displayed in Google's SERPs. You may wish to edit your Web sites Title tag and/or its Description Meta tag after viewing this.

- **Subscriber Stats** – Google now owns ww.feedburner .com and allows feed (e.g., RSS, Atom, etc.) subscription monitoring, via this tool.

Web Site Links

If you knew what Web pages currently linked to your Web site's pages, you could cater the SEO copy (text) on your Web pages to better suit the traffic coming from these sites, right? That is exactly what the statistics from this tool allows you to do. You can also see what pages on your site have no inbound links and take corrective action.

- **Pages with External Links** – When deciding whether to change or delete a Web page, check the pages with the external links section of the *Google Webmaster Tools Links* tool first. You will avoid dramatic visitor traffic and page rank changes that way.

- **Pages with Internal Links** – When deciding whether to change or delete a Web page, check the pages with internal links section of the *Google Webmaster Tools Links* tool first. You will avoid creating dead links and potential Web page availability issues that way. This can also sometimes dramatically affect your SEO, especially if a heavily linked Web page is involved.

- **Site-links** – Google automatically generates site links to aid users of its search tools. These are completely automated and based on an algorithm that decides based on the structure and content of your Web site. A sitemap dramatically increases your chances of being included. The Site-links section shows you site links currently available for your Web site.

Site Maps

We have already covered this in an earlier chapter; *See page* 24. This is the section where you can add and resubmit your sitemaps. If you have not done so already, I advise you to do so at your earliest convenience.

Tools

Finally, Google Webmaster Tools also provides many features for checking, verifying, fine-tuning, and enhancing your Web site. Let us briefly look at some of the current tools.

- *Analyze Robots.txt* – shows you the contents of your robots.txt file and allows you to check if Googlebot and Google user-agents (Googlebot-Mobile, Googlebot-Image, MediaPartners-Google, and Adsbot-Google, have access to specific links within your Web site. Note that MediaPartners-Google, and Adsbot-Google are user-agents used by Google to crawl for AdSense and AdWords, respectively.

- *Manage Site Verification* – allows you to verify your Web sites with Google Webmaster Tools.

- *Set Crawl Rate* – view statistical data for the last 90 days about how Googlebot has crawled your Web pages and the speeds involved. If the Googlebot is causing your Web site to be slower than you would like, you can set the crawl rate to a slower rate.

> **WARNING:**
> Setting your crawl rate to a slower rate will reduce the number of times and frequency that the Googlebot visits. This may be an issue if you have content that changes frequently.

- **Set Geographic Target** – Change the geographic target for your Web site. This tool allows you to change the country you wish your Web site to be specifically targeted at. There are no guarantees for accuracy by Google. However, this may allow your Web site to be more focused to a geographic region. The default is "Do not associate a geographic location with this site".

> **WARNING:**
> You can only select one country; and doing so may greatly limit the traffic you receive. Therefore, unless you really need to, I would advise you leave this setting on the default.

- **Set Preferred Domain** – Allows you to associate the various representations of your Web domain, e.g., "www.practicalbooks.org" and "practicalbooks.org". You can select to associate all to one, or not to associate any of them at all.

- **Enable Enhanced Image Search** – Enabling this feature allows Google to crawl your Web site for images to use in its image search.

> **WARNING:**
> Enabling enhanced image search will cause the Googlebot-image-user-agent to frequent your Web site. This will increase the traffic on your Web server and could be an issue if you have a high amount of images, or if your site is relatively large.

- **Remove URLs** – Allows you to remove a page, directory or a Web site from the Google index. This takes effect after ninety days and within that period can revoke your request. You are advised to make sure the content is no longer live on your site and an 'HTTP 404 Not Found', or a '410' status code, is displayed when the page is accessed, before using the META NOINDEX tag or robots.txt file to block the file, directory or entire site. The *Remove URLs* tool allows you to remove files, directories or subdirectories, an entire Web site or a cached copy of a Google search result from the Google index, or cache servers.

WARNING:
This is a powerful and dangerous tool. Be sure to tread carefully and know exactly what you are removing before proceeding.

- *Gadgets* – Allows you to add Google Webmaster Tools to your iGoogle profile. A more useful set of free gadgets for adding functionality, interest and potentially improving your Web site visitor retention may be found at www.google.com/ig/directory?synd=open&source.

Google Analytics

Google offers a free monitoring tool called Google Analytics at www.google.com/analytics. We will be using this tool exclusively throughout this section. If your Web site sits behind a firewall or if you want the secured knowledge that your Web site statistics details is in your full control, then you can download and install Urchin 5 (or Urchin 6 when it is available).

Urchin 5 and/or Urchin 6 is a tool that gathers the same statistical data about your Web site traffic; however, unlike Google Analytics which gathers statistical data which you view and create reports from, (within your Google Analytics account), Urchin 5 and Urchin 6 provide this functionality from your Web server. Therefore, you cut Google Analytics out and maintain the service yourself.

Unfortunately, Urchin 5 and the new Urchin 6 are not free. They come with a 30-day demo; however, after 30 days you will need to purchase a licence if you wish to continue using the software. I will not discuss Urchin 5 or Urchin 6 in this section, as we will be using Google Analytics exclusively.

For further information on, and to download the Urchin 5 or Urchin 6 software, go to the following links:

- www.google.com/analytics/urchin_software.html
- www.google.com/analytics/urchin_downloads.html

If you want a third party qualified Google Analytics support partner to help you setup and use the Google Analytics service, visit the following link:

- www.google.com/analytics/support_partner_provided.html

The Google Analytics tool can help you identify what marketing copy attracts visitors the most; it can also help you identify what landing pages are working best for you. One of the most useful features of Google Analytics is the seemless integration with Google AdWords. This allows it to view your return on investment (ROI) data, without having to import or key-in cost details.

Google Analytics is highly scaleable and is actually used by Google themselves. It can also be used to track all advertisement campaigns, including e-mail ads and ads from different search engines and referral sources.

Getting Started with Google Analytics

To get started, sign up to the Google Analytics service at (www.google.com/analytics/sign_up.html). If you already have a Google account you can use that to log in, then sign up to the Google Analytics service. You can use www.google.com/analytics/home/provision/ to sign up to the Google Analytics service in your Google account.

As part of the sign up process, you will be presented with a page requesting your Web site name, the Google Analytics account name (it's suggested you call it by your Web site name), your phone number and country or territory. After filling in this simple form, click continue. You will be taken to a page with your Google Analytics code in JavaScript or the old legacy Urchin script.

Copy the preferred script (JavaScript recommended) and have your Web master add it to your Web site HTML code. You must add it to every page that you want to monitor using Google Analytics.

If you have previously added the legacy code to some of your Web pages, you need to remove the legacy code first, before adding the new JavaScript code; otherwise your Google Analytics metrics will be inaccurate.

Now you are ready to Check the Status of your Web site. Google analytics checks the home page of your Web site to determine if the Google Analytics code has been added to it. If it is not present, you will receive this error message, "Tracking not yet added to your Web site: [your website address]".

Add the JavaScript code to your Web pages including your home page and click the 'Check Status' button again. "Waiting for Data" will be displayed and underneath this message will read, "Analytics has been successfully installed and data is being gathered now". At the bottom of the page you'll see 'Tracking Status Information'; click the "Finish" button.

You will be taken to the Analytics Settings page. Listed under the Web site profile will be all your Web pages with the JavaScript code inserted. After installing Google Analytics code and clicking on the 'Check Status' button, it could take up to twenty-four hours for your Web site pages to be listed.

While waiting for the details to appear, you can click on the 'View Reports' link in the upper left-hand side of the Analytics Settings. But before we go into this, let us look at a few other things on the Analytics Settings page.

Add Web Site Profile Link

This link will take you to the Analytics Account Creation window. Use this link if you want to add another Web site to your Google Analytics account.

Access Manager Link

You will see all the user accounts that have access to your Google Analytics account. You may add more users (with the + Add User link) or delete current users with the "delete" link next to their e-mail account details. You are not allowed to delete the administrator account, if it is the only account shown.

When adding accounts you can select to give them "Administrator" account privileges or "View Reports Only" account privileges. When you have finished, click "Finish" or use the navigation links at the top left-hand window to return to the Analytics Settings.

Filter Manager link

Your Web site might have a robot or another Web site monitoring or frequently accessing it. You may not want this site included in the statistics that Google Analytics reports on. You can use the Filter Manager to filter out traffic from this domain, an IP address from a subdirectory of the same Web site, or use a custom filter with a lot more detailed setting. This is an extremely powerful function. You can even set the case sensitivity of the filter details.

Give the filters you create logical names, so that you can easily identify and know what they are doing from their name alone. Failure to do this will cause you to edit the filter to see what each one does whenever you want to remove or amend one.

Helpful Links

In the Analytics Settings page, to the far right, you will find "Helpful Links". There are many useful help pages there. Read through them while you wait for your Web site data to be collected by Google Analytics. Try the "Take a Tour" link to familiarize yourself with the features.

Web Site Profiles Settings

How do you determine when a sale has been made or when a successful selection or action has been taken by a visitor to your Web site? You use goals. In Google Analytics, goals are used to capture actions or results. For instance, if you wanted to know when a visitor has successfully purchased a product, you could set a goal on the landing page that successful sales return to. Therefore, any visits to this page show up in your statistics as a successful sale. You can set up goals to track any page that you wish to monitor traffic.

Let us look at how a goal is set up in Google Analytics. In Analytics Settings, under the Web site Profiles section, select the edit link next to the landing page for a successful sale, or a successful e-mail address submission, as an example.

You will be taken to the profile settings for the page. You are allowed four goals per profile page. Select the Edit link against the first goal. You will be taken to Goal Settings: G1.

In the next page, "Enter Goal Information" and "Define Funnel (optional)" sections are presented. To fill in the goal details start with Match Type. Click the question mark next to Match Type to get an explanation of each type. Next, fill in the Goal URL (remember the Match Type, therefore, use the correct URL i.e., partial, head matched or full URL).

Now give your goal a name. This name will appear in the conversion reports; use a name that is easy to relate to the goal, or conversion. Again you can specify if the goal details are case sensitive or not.

You need to know the drop off rate leading to a goal; i.e., how many people start off looking like they were going to buy, but never got to the landing page. This could be useful data. It could point to one particular page being the cause of many lost sales. With this knowledge you could rewrite the copy on that page, or illiminate the step that is adversely affecting your sales.

To do this, after setting up the goal with the goal information, you can define funnel details. The "Define Funnel (optional)" section is used for this. Input the path taken to reach the target goal page; however, do not include the goal page in your funnel steps settings. You can set the first step page in the funnel as mandatory by selecting the [required step] box, next to the first step name. Doing this means that the step page must be visited before the goal page for the goal to be counted in the "Funnel Visualization report". We shall discuss this report and others shortly. After you complete setting up the funnel steps click on the "Save Changes" button.

After setting up all your goals for the Web site profile, you can add filters specifically to this profile or apply the general one setup for the Web site to this profile.

Google Analytics Reports

Click on "view reports" at the top, left-hand of the Analytics Settings page. You will be taken to the "Dashboard". This is your main Google Analytics reports page. You will see a quick summary of your site's usage, visitor overview, map overlay, traffic sources overview and content overview. You can click on the "view reports" under each of these highlights to see the full, associated report. Or, use the links on the far left pane. View metrics and settings under "Visitors", "Traffic Sources", "Content" and "Goals".

You can also set an e-mail address to send reports to or export reports to a PDF, XML, CSV, TSV file or e-mail. If sending via e-mail, you also have a choice of sending to yourself, others, and/or sending as a PDF, XML, CSV or TSV file format(s). You can also set up a scheduled report via e-mail. The schedule can be daily (report is sent in the morning), weekly, monthly, or quarterly (the report is sent on the first day of the period).

The reporting capabilities of Google Analytics is truly outstanding for the fact that it is offered free of charge.

On the Dashboard you are immediately presented with Visits, Pageviews, Pages/visit, Bounce Rate, Avg. Time on Site and %New Visits. This is the default setting of the Dashboard; however you can change this by adding or removing metrics from the Dashboard.

You can click on each metric on the far left-hand pane and explore them at a more detailed level.

To the far right, near the top, on the Dashboard, you will see displayed the date range being viewed. Using the drop down next to this date range you can select to compare two periods such as the current month with the next month. You can also choose to compare the report against the site performance report.

Under the comparison section, you can change the mode of the graph on the Dashboard. Select to see just one metric, compare two metrics or compare a metric in a date range. The overview and overlay panes on the Dashboard can be removed with the crosses in the top right-hand corner of each box.

I have offered you here a brief overview of the Google Analytics tool. For more in-depth help and explanation of each feature, variable and metric, visit https://www.google.com/support/googleanalytics. To find out more about reports click on the Report Finder link at the bottom right-hand pane of the Dashboard page.

Fine-Tuning

In this section we shall take many of the Google Analytics metrics and see how they point to issues that may require fine-tuning with your Web site, advertising or SEO.

Bounce Rate

If you are getting a high bounce rate, it may point to misleading links, misleading advertising, poor referrals or it could point to a really poor Web site that puts visitors off at the first glance.

One way to correct this problem is to look at where these visitors are coming from. It could be that they are all being sent from one source. In Google Analytics, check the "Traffic Sources Overview" page. Perhaps a blog, directory listing, search engine submission, social networking page, news article, press release or a Google AdWords advertisement is set-up, misleading visitors to think your Web page holds something that they don't find once they arrive.

If the problem lies with a Google AdWords advertisement, it may be targeting the wrong audience through inaccurate or ineffective keywords. Knowing this, you can change the advertisement. If an affiliate or other referrer is sending you poor hits, you can identify that and remove the source with a filter in Google Analytics. You can also deal with the affiliate or referrer accordingly.

Lastly, if you discover that it is not a problem with the sources of the visitors, you can only assume your landing page or Web site is putting visitors off. You can then proceed to set up some polls, surveys or market research to identify what they dislike the most about the site- and change it.

Conversion Rate

We have already covered the setting up of goals and funnels within Google Analytics to capture conversions and traffic flow towards conversion. Every Web site that sells something or seeks to get something from visitors should be interested in knowing what their conversion rate is.

Google Analytics provides this service through goals and funnels. After setting up your goals and funnels, you can view your conversion rate under "Goals", in the Analytics Settings left-hand pane. You can also view a visual representation of your funnels and the flow of traffic through them towards the conversion point. Goal conversion metrics can also be accessed for AdWare campaigns within the AdWare group.

Click Overlay

The Click Overlay Tool shows you an image of your Web site with click data overlaid on top. This is a highly effective visual tool that shows you where people like to click on your Web pages. It could provide you with essential information of where to place sales links on your site.

Pages per Visit

Bounce rate highlights serious retention issues with your sight, however, a less obvious problem is picked up by the Pages/Visit metric; visitors coming to your Web site and only looking at a few pages before leaving. This could be due to all the same reasons as was given for Bounce Rate, however this situation could also be due to a highly effective landing page leading to immediate conversions.

If conversion rates from the Goals section of Google Analytics do not support the effective landing page proposition, then you need to turn to funnels to determine where you are mostly losing these visitors. If a pattern emerges pointing to a particular page or pages, you should analyze the copy of those pages and have them re-written to improve the visitor retention.

Average Time on Site

A high page view, pages/visit, and avg. time on site metric that is not supported by high conversion-to-sales rate, might imply that visitors are having difficulty finding out how to buy on your site. It could also mean that visitors are finding useful information or entertainment on your Web site that is preventing them from converting to buyers.

Use Google Analytics to set up funnels. From the funnels, you will identify which pages cause the most deviation from the conversion path. That is, you will identify where, along the way to a sale, your visitors are getting distracted. You can solve this quickly by rewriting the copy on that page(s), remove those pages or combine them to avoid too many stops on the way to conversion. Experiment with each solution until you eliminate the problem.

Per Cent New Visits

A healthy Web site should have more new visitor conversions than previous visitor conversions. Therefore, if your % New Visits metric is low, it could spell a problem in attracting new visitors. Perhaps you are offering a service that requires users to revisit your site regularly to access their account, or otherwise use your service.

If that is the case, the low % New Visit figure might not be a problem, however if this is not the case, then you may need to re-evaluate your advertising and marketing plan. Try pay-per-click with Google AdWords and revisit all the SEO points raised in this book to see how your Web site could utilize them.

Keyword Positions

If you are trying to improve your keyword ranking on search engines, you will be glad to know that Google Analytics provides this metric for your Web pages. You can identify what keywords bring you the most conversions. This can save you a lot of marketing and SEO time. Knowing what is already working best for you can empower and provide you with the knowledge to improve what is proving to work well. Similarly, the keywords that are not aiding in conversions should be dropped in favor of those that are working.

The metric is available in the Traffic Sources section, and again within the AdWare group for monitoring AdWare ads keyword positions.

Traffic Sources

After carrying out so much SEO activity, you want to know if any of it has been effective. If you carry out SEO to improve your rank at a particular search engine or a group of them, you can use Google Analytics to see if your traffic sources metrics are showing any improvement in traffic sent by search engines.

You are not limited to Search engines alone, you can use Google Analytics to track traffic sent from any source. Within the Traffic Sources section, select 'Referring Sites' to track the sites that are referring traffic to your Web site. You can see how efficient this traffic is being on your Web site with the Visits, Pages /Visit, Avg. Time on Site, % New Visits and Bounce Rates. You can isolate referrers using the 'Find Source' filter tool at the bottom of the Referring Sites page.

You can also use the "Show" and "Segment" section(s) within the pages in Traffic Sources to identify: paid or non-paid, source, medium, campaign, keyword, ad content, visitor type, landing page, browser, language and other geographical attributes relating to the referred traffic.

Tracking Google AdWords

I mentioned earlier that built into Google Analytics is an AdWords monitoring and reporting functionality. This feature allows you to view Google AdWords campaigns and their various metrics, view the goal conversions associated with ad campaigns, and monitor a host of other metrics. Some of the metrics this gives you the ability to monitor are as follows:

- Impressions
- Clicks
- Cost
- Average click-through rate (ctr)
- Average cost-per-click (cpc)
- Average revenue-per-click (rpc)
- Return on investment (roi)
- Margin ([e-commerce revenue + total goal value – cost] divided by revenue)

The cost, CPC, ROI, and CTR are perhaps the most used Goggle AdWare metrics by Web masters. Keep your eye on these to help control your costs.

Visitor Segmentation

If you need to identify what browser software your visitors use, or what operating system, screen resolution, screen colors, java support, flash, language, or network location they belong to, Google Analytics can report on these also. Under the Visitors tab you will find the metrics for all these and more.

This information is useful to improve your Web site support for visitor software, screen resolution and geographic location. We spoke earlier about supporting multiple languages with your Web site. With the Google Analytics map overlay, you will get a graphical representation of the network locations of your visitors. This should help you identify where the majority of your foreign visitors are coming from, making it easier to identify the language(s) to investigate providing support for.

Within the Visitor section, you can also access metrics for Visitor Trending, Visitor Loyalty and comparison of New vs. Returning Visitors.

Web Site Optimizer

If you want to experiment with different designs and content for your Web site in a controlled and monitored environment, you can use the Google AdWords tool, Web site Optimizer. The tool is accessible through Google Analytics but requires login to Google AdWare to use.

Web site Optimizer is currently in Beta testing, however it promises to be extremely successful and useful for Web site optimization. It basically aims to improve conversion rates. Whether you are looking for more sales, more e-mail enquiries, download or any other call to action from visitors, this tool can help you identify the best way to make changes to your Web site to achieve better results.

By placing special code within your HTML code, you allow Google Web site Optimizer to make controlled changes of headings, images, conversion links and other sections of your Web pages looking to identify what combination results in the most conversions. After identifying the configuration which causes the most successful conversion rates, you can simply apply the changed code directly to your Web site.

The tool comes with two options depending on how much traffic you currently get to your site. For hits below 1000 per week, the A/B testing solution is advised, while for hit rates above 1000 the Multivariate testing solution is advised.

The difference between the two is that the A/B uses single changes at a time, while the Multivariate can accommodate many changes to the Web page at the same time. To learn more about this exciting tool, visit the training links below:

- http://services.google.com/training/websiteoptimizerabsetup/2995105/indexhtml
- http://services.google.com/training/websiteoptimizeroverview/2995095/index.html
- http://services.google.com/training/websiteoptimizeruserguide

Other features

Google is constantly adding features and tools to its Analytics. Make sure you check regularly for new changes.

Site Search

If your Web site offers a search facility, Google Analytics can monitor what visitors search for, where they go most often after a search, and where they search from. This can be vital SEO information for you to maximize the most popular pages visited after searches. This tool also informs you of what product groups people searched for the most.

You will find the Site Search feature and metrics under the Content section on the left pane of the Analytics Settings page.

Top Exits and Top Landing Pages

The pages that are used to enter and leave your Web site are critical to know meticulously well. Within Google Analytics you can find these under Content. "Top Landing Pages" shows the URLs of the pages used to enter your Web site in order of most entrances against bounces and bounce rates.

Similarly, for "Top Exit Pages", Page views and % Exit metrics are presented. It is important to know what these pages are so that you can address why they are so popularly used for exiting your site. Perhaps you could rewrite them or add content to draw the visitors back into the site, and towards the conversion pages.

Chapter 6

Promotion & Advertising

Other Promotion Mediums

So far we have looked at many SEO, advertising and promotion techniques and methods; however, there are many other ways of promoting your business, Web site or feed. In this chapter we look at many offline (and a few online) mediums for promoting your Web site. The following are mediums through which you could promote your Web site:

- Amazon.com and online bookstores
- Applications and applets
- Articles for magazines
- Articles for online sites
- Audio books
- Billboard/posters
- Continuity programs
- E-Books
- E-Courses
- E-Zines
- Google Book Search
- Live conferences
- Newspapers
- Newspapers and magazines
- Physical Book
- Podcasts
- Press releases
- Print on demand publishing: lulu.com, Amazon BookSurge
- Public places
- Radio
- Retreats
- Social networking
- Speeches
- Tele-class
- Tele-seminar
- Television
- Vehicle wrapping
- Video/DVDs

- Web logs, video logs, photo logs and mobile phone logs
- Webinars
- Workbook
- Workshops

This list can be broken into the following categories:

1) Digital products (applet and application downloads, blogs, photo-blogs, vlogs, podcasts, webinars, e-courses, e-books, e-zines): are distributed via an Internet strategy.
2) Physical products (articles for magazines, physical books, audio books, DVDs, print on demand publishing, newspapers and magazines): require a physical distribution strategy.
3) Training products (live conferences, recordings of tele-classes, retreats, speeches, tele-classes, tele-seminars, workshops and workbooks): are distributed through a course/training strategy.
4) Continuity programs incorporate some of these mediums.
5) Conventional advertising (billboards, posters, newspapers, magazines, press releases, public places, radio, television and vehicle wrapping): use the conventional marketing mediums.

Let us look at these categories individually and discuss some of the included mediums in more detail.

Digital Products

We have already covered applet and application downloads, blogs, photo-blogs, vlogs, mo-blogs, podcasts applets and software downloads; now we shall look at e-courses, e-books, e-zines and webinar downloads.

E-Courses

E-Courses are electronic courses. They can be held online or offline. When run offline they tend to either be on CD/DVD or via stored files on a computer. When online, e-courses can be hosted on interactive training Web sites, through streaming movies, presentations, online viewable documents, or a mixture of some or all the above. The offline versions can be just as varied and dynamic however, you do not need an Internet connection to use them.

Offline e-courses are limited to simple advertising and promotion of your service, Web site and/or brand; although you can be much more dynamic in the marketing of your Web site, service, or product on an online e-course. If the sole purpose of the course is to promote your Web site, i.e., SEO purposes, then you could create an e-course and offer it free of charge to Web masters and Web users.

Making your course into a product that Web masters can integrate into their Web sites, embed or link to, will promote your site and provide back-links. This way, the candidates of the courses will can link to you. Furthermore, provide a service such as www.addthis.com to help promote your course on social networking sites and blogs.

To fully utilize the various social mediums available to you, make sure your course Web site offers images, streaming video and MP3 files which can be added to online articles. Clearly state that the content is *free* and can be distributed as long as a link to your Web site is always included.

To learn how to create and market an online e-course, see the following links:

E-COURSE RESOURCES	
Creating online/offline tutorials & presentations:	www.librarysupportstaff.com/presentations.html
e-Course tools:	www.c4lpt.co.uk/Directory http://moodle.org
e-Learning management system provider:	www.coursemaker.co.uk www.eleapsoftware.com www.udutu.com
Directory to advertise your e-course:	www.ecourseweb.com

Table 7: E-Course Resources

Whether you are using an adobe acrobat text with embedded images document, Microsoft PowerPoint document, or a slick, fully integrated interactive Web solution for your training course, make sure you follow the basic SEO rules – correctly title and fully utilize tags and META tags.

Theme your document, presentation or Web page and select a theme that aligns title and description text to the left. Include your Web site address on each page and include your Web site address in sound (vocally), images (visually) and video (with a permanent visual banner or footer like the YouTube logo on all YouTube videos, as well as at the beginning and end credits).

E-Books

Electronic books (or e-books) are another way to promote your Web site, service, product or business. Sites such as Amazon Kindle (www.kindle.com), Mobipocket, found at (www.mobipocket.com/ebookbase), Lulu (www.lulu .com), Café Press (www.cafepress.com), Lightning Source (www.lightningsource.com) and many others, provide free e-book production, distribution and sales services.

Like the e-courses discussed previously, if you want to get your e-book into as many handhelds, laptops, mobile devices, PDAs, Tablet PCs, Smartphone's and computers as possible, you have to offer it for free. To do this, you have to first create an excellent e-book on a topic related to your Web site. Throughout the pages of the e-book and also on the cover and in the description text, include your Web site address.

Every time someone features the e-book on their Web site, or views it on their computer or mobile device, they will see your Web site address and read how your Web site can assist them in achieving the objective covered by the e-book. You can create several versions.

An electronic book can use all the same headings and setup as a normal book, however, because it is in the electronic format, you can use bookmarks, links, contracted and exploded bullet points, etc. Learn more about how to create an effective e-book and distribute it from the following links:

E-Book Store Creation

- E-book conversion sites: https://www.mobipocket.com/ebookbase/en/homepage/conversion.asp
- www.amazon.com
- www.cafepress.com
- www.froogle.com
- www.google.com/base
- www.lulu.com
- www.make-a-store.com

Organizations

- http://gutenberg.net.au
- http://ibiblio.org
- www.gutenberg.cc
- www.librivox.org
- www.literalsystems.org
- www.worldlibrary.net

Distribution

- http://books.google.com
- www.audiobooksforfree.com
- www.lightningsource.com
- www.mobilebooks.org

E-Book Marketing

- www.guidetoebookmarketing.com

E-Book Creation

- www.ebookswriter.com
- www.yudu.com
- Search for "ebook [creation tools] [publishers] [distribution][store] [conversion]" on any major search engine

You can also create audio e-books. Revisit the section on Podcasts; *See page* 88 for a more effective way of promoting your Web site, product or service with audio broadcasts. The following are links to audio e-book resources:

Audiobook Creation

- www.audiobookcreator.com
- *Also see page* 88

Retailers and Distributers

- www.amazon.com
- www.audible.com
- www.pickabook.co.uk

Alternatively, search for "audio e-book creation" or "how to make an audio e-book" on any major search engine.

E-Zines

A newsletter can be a useful tool for gathering members, supporters or fans of your product, service or Web site. You can use the medium to remind them of your offerings, advertise other things, (whether your own or paying advertiser's endorse things); announce the new "material" or tease them about upcoming "goodies", whatever they may be.

While offline newsletters are effective in their own right, they cost more to print and distribute (especially if you are offering them for free). The online e-zine costs less to produce and even less to distribute. You can deliver it via e-mail, blog or a download from your Web site. You can syndicate the e-zine from your Web site and deliver it through RSS or Atom.

Like all mediums, your e-zine needs to be targeted to the demographic of interest. No need in your e-zines targeting students and stay home mothers if your Web site is selling racecars or stock trading software. Make sure you first understand the target market of your Web site, before finding out what that market would be interested to read in an e-zine.

Use an Internet marketing company (i.e., www.know this.com or http://directory.esomar.org) to find this information out for you or, do it yourself using questionnaires, polls and directly asking your current customers what they would like to see in an e-zine (or if they would like an e-zine at all).

You should also find out what medium they would prefer to receive the e-zine through and the frequency of editions. In some cases, your customers and target market would actually be prepared to pay for such an e-zine.

Once you know what your target market wants to see and read in an e-zine, create one for them. You can do it all yourself or recruit the help of article writers and an e-zine editor from a freelance site such as www.ifreelance.com or www.guru.com. You could also write and ask your favorite newsletter writers if they would be interested in helping with your newsletter project.

Next, name your e-zine. It's a good idea to include the name of your Web site in the name of the e-zine. The name should also indicate that this is a periodical. Decide on a numbering convention. You can use whatever you want however, "Issue X, Volume X" where "X" is a number, is the standard. Decide on the format of the e-zine, and a logo.

Before setting out to write your e-zine, you should know what your Web site's best selling points are, who your customers and target market are, any recent product or service launches (these by themselves could be the core of an e-zine edition), any recent awards to your Web site, testimonials from customers of your site, what industry news has been released, and any significant changes planned to your Web site or how a past change went.

The e-zine can also be used to straighten image problems and misconceptions of your service or products held by customers. You can also have polls, quizzes, prize drawings and competitions, cartoon strips, funny stories submitted by readers, etc.

You can set out your e-zine using a template from Microsoft Publisher, Microsoft Word or a Web authoring software such as Microsoft FrontPage. You can convert it to a PDF file afterwards if you have Adobe Acrobat Writer. Try www.primopdf.com and www.dopdf.com for free software that writes to PDF files.

Keeping the target audience in mind, decide which items from the list below what you could use in your e-zine:

1) Ads and endorsements
2) Boilerplate paragraph as footer
3) Cartoon strips
4) Columns
5) Coming-attraction ads
6) Cover
7) Editorials
8) Feature articles
9) Funny stories
10) Good news/success stories
11) Masthead
12) New product announcements
13) News articles
14) Personality profiles
15) Photos and images
16) Polls
17) Prize draws and competitions
18) Q&A
19) Quizzes
20) Subscription link
21) Table of contents

Start with the headlines for the various stories and articles. Decide on the contents and set out a contents page. Map out the items to the columns and sections of your e-zine. Try not to clutter the pages of the e-zine. Have three to six items per page. Use different type face and font sizes for pull quotes[2]. Use images to enhance the look and feel of the pages. These also help draw reader's eyes.

Have a headline for every article and a caption for every photo. Use a boilerplate that explains the mission of your e-zine at the bottom of each page and a header containing the issue date, issue and volume number, as well as page number and e-zine title.

---

[2] A snippet of the content made to stand out from the text to grab a readers attention.

Your articles should encourage readers to send e-mails to comment, enquire, complain, agree, sign-up, etc. Use the polls, quizzes, prize draws, Q&As and funny stories to gather information from the readers. Collect name and e-mail addresses and other contact details. This is your database of potential future customers.

At least 20% of the e-zine should promote your Web site, service or product. Syndicate the e-zine. Revisit page 84 for details on how to setup feeds. Each page should contain a subscription link as well as a social bookmarking link (see www.addthat.com).You can also have advertisements from paying advertisers, or endorsements and self advertising about your Web site throughout the e-zine. Have at least one advertisement per page promoting your Web site. However, do not over do this.

Create a mailing list of customers and others who have agreed to receive the e-zine. Remember, do not send spam or you will undo all your good work. Over time, as your mailing list grows, you can send regular promotional emails about special offers, sales, events, new features, etc., to your mailing list. Each mailing should also promote your Web site(s).

Finally, check and recheck your spelling and grammar. Have others check this for you as well. Confirm all supporting statements and quotes and acquire permission to use any details, photos or images in your e-zine. The following are useful links for publishing, distributing and advertising your e-zine:

RSS Feed Creation:

- http://rss.icerocket.com
- www.mysitefeed.com
- www.rss-info.com/RSSeditor-v09-54-setup.exe

E-Zine Publishers:

- http://emailuniverse.com
- http://ezinearticles.com
- http://new-list.com
- https://www.ezinedirector.com
- www.ezine.com

- www.ezine-dir.com
- www.lulu.com

Webinars

A webinar is an Internet-based seminar. Just like a normal seminar, attendees have to be present at a certain time (if they want to have interactive access to the speakers), however, unlike normal seminars, the attendees do not need to be in the same geographic vicinity of the speakers. In fact, they could be continents apart.

Attendees access the seminar via computer, sound and video equipment and can listen to the speaker or other sound presentations, watch video or graphical presentations, and read seminar notes or other supporting material while the seminar commences.

Because the attendees do not need to be within the same building as the speaker, the speaker can be in a studio or other venue where the webinar is being filmed. All he might need is a computer or laptop with all the supporting materials, microphone, teleprompter notes and video camera(s) to capture his presentation.

Attendees sit at their computers or laptops and log into the seminar via the Internet. They could have a webcam on their machine so the speaker can see them or not. They can ask questions by typing their questions on their keyboard for the speaker to read, or they can use their microphone and ask questions directly to the speaker.

Webinars are a great way of promoting your Web site. Unlike offline seminars, you are not restricted to how many seats a venue can hold. You can also record your webinars and make it available to attendees at a later time or date. The recorded versions will not allow trainer/speaker interaction. However this facility bridges time zone issues and allows attendees to attend the webinar, pause it and continue at a later date. In some cases, attendees can also rewind and fast forward recorded webinars.

Giving a seminar on a subject related to your product, service or Web site can be a powerful way of selling and promoting your products, services and Web site. What could be better than an attentive audience right in front of you?

There are many ways of presenting webinars; from simple webcams, webinar software and PowerPoint presentations on your laptop, to full studio support with camera crew, sound crew and support staff vetting questions from attendees. The following are sources of webinar services and software.

- http://meetingrooms.regus.co.uk
- http://podia.net/p.aspx?a=1169
- https://www1.gotowebinar.com
- www.coursemaker.co.uk/
- www.megameeting.com
- www.netviewer.co.uk
- www.presenternet.com
- www.webex.com/overview/webinars.html

The key to a successful webinar or seminar is the preparation, presentation, delivery and Q&A session at the end. Ultimately, your aim is to get buy-ins for your product or service from the attendees. You can judge your success in doing so by how many sales or sign ups you make from the webinar, or how many contact details you collect from attendees.

Preparation

Like all presentations, the better you prepare the better you will be able to deliver your presentation and answer questions from attendees afterwards. You will also understand your subject better and understand how you can link sections of your talk together seamlessly.

Before you start to prepare the actual talk, do your research. Make sure you understand your audience, their requirements, desires and needs, local or cultural differences as well as learning ability and expected concentration levels. This will determine whether to include boring technical detail or to summarize these and move on to other more exciting presentations and sections of your talk.

Avoid surprises; thoroughly familiarize yourself with your subject matter. Will you be using any supporting technology, materials or multimedia presentations? Make sure you familiarize yourself with all supporting material and equipment. You do not want to start learning to use a piece of software or pointing tool on the actual day of the webinar.

Create notes for your talk, however, do not write these verbatim. Use pointers to jog your memory on what you will be covering in each section. Also make notes on transition – how you will move from one subject or part of the talk to another.

Use video, sound, pictures and images with color to jazz up your talk and keep attendees interested. Avoid speaking in a monotone. Use inflection, volume, questions and hand and facial expressions to create variety in your talk. This stops monotonic, boring and lifeless presenting.

Practice in front of a mirror, record yourself and replay it back to analyze and improve your delivery. Once you have completed your research and preparation you can start preparing the actual presentation.

Presentation and Delivery

Your presentation should always begin with your introduction followed by what you are going to discuss. You can set out the format of your talk at this stage, explaining how long the talk should be and the expected end time. You can also advise the audience to bookmark your Web site link for later. Get the audience involved with a poll, i.e., ask where attendees are from, their level of knowledge or understanding of the subject matter, etc. This quick, simple poll relaxes people and gets them feeling more involved, it may actually also give you vital last minute research to fine tune your talk.

Be careful not to start vetting questions at this stage though. Explain that there will be opportunities to ask questions at the end or at designated points within the talk. You may need to explain some technical details about how attendees can access supporting material; view video, files and see pictures, etc., or how to submit questions, or use their webinar software.

Have a handkerchief, tissue paper and a glass of water near by. If using a microphone, make sure it is adjusted correctly before you proceed into the presentation.

You are now ready to begin. Start with the title and objectives of the webinar. Take each objective in turn and deliver your talk accordingly, including supporting materials, where necessary.

Theme your presentation, select soft or warm colors as the theme colors and set the titles and headings as well as the sub headings to the left. Make sure you have your Web site name and address wherever appropriate. It could be a logo on each slide, a backdrop for the video presentation of the webinar and on all supporting material. If possible, use a Web link rather than an unlinked graphical image. A linked image or text allows attendees to link to your Web site.

Do not use timings on your presentation. You control the time- not the presentation. This is to avoid going out of synch with your presentation. If you control the pace of the presentation, you will never have to worry about being out of synch. Always end each section with a question or problem which will be answered by the topic of the next section.

When using slides, always make a comment or statement as you click or bring on the next slide. Never pause while waiting for the slide to come on. At the end of each section, wrap up the section by summarizing what you have covered in that section.

Within reason, you should only spend a minute and a half per slide. This is not a hard rule as you may require spending longer or shorter in some special cases, however, on average a minute and a half should be sufficient to explain each slide.

At the end of the seminar summarize the entire talk again and move to the Q&A section and accept questions from the audience or attendees.

Q&A Section

This is where you take questions from attendees. This could be in the form of text messaging, e-mail, phone calls or via voice over IP (VOIP), through the webinar software. Whichever way you do it, keep your answers brief, to the point and accurate. Don't use this time to start another seminar.

Decide before-hand how many questions you will field or how long the Q&A session will last. Keep to these limits and thank the attendees for their attention and attendance and end the session.

Physical Products

We shall now look at how you can use offline products such as books, audio books, articles for newspapers and magazines, DVDs and seminars to promote your Web site.

Book

In the first part of this book I referred heavily to www.practicalbooks.org and www.samuelblankson.com. This was done to highlight and help explain this next section, promoting your Web site through books. Although e-books and other electronic formats have encroached on the book market, books still dominate as the preferred medium for reading literature and text.

When your Web site is endorsed or referred to in a book, the reader may check it out if it is essential to their study, or if they are curious when a Web site or service is continuously referred to in a book: and the Web site is an intrinsic part of the book, with additional support material available only from the Web site, the reader has no option but to visit the Web site.

This is the key to book promotion; you either get yourself mentioned many times in a book, relating to your Web site content, service or products or you can write a book about your specialty and heavily feature the Web site in it. Such shameless promotion books are more often vanity pressed or printed through Print on Demand (PoD). This is because it is unlikely that a conventional publishing house would endorse such a book.

Another consideration is time to publication. With PoD, lead time to publication can be measured in months rather than years with a conventional publisher. This includes finding a publisher, if you currently do not have one. The book writing process is a complex one. Further detail will be covered shortly, however, it can be broken down into three main categories: the book research, book writing and book marketing processes, as follows:

Step 1 Research	• Market Research • Content Research
Step 2 Publishing	• Content Writing • Content Editing
Step 3 Marketing	• Promotiong • Marketing

The book research and book writing steps make up the book publishing process, while the marketing of the finished book is the domain of the book marketing process.

Book Publishing Process

- Market Research: Discover what readers want; what is currently popular, the format, length and then decide upon your content.

- Content Research: Outline the content of your book; research the subject matter and gather pertinent supporting materials. In the end, you may or may not use all of the data you have gathered, but it is usually best to thoroughly cover your subject(s).

- Content Writing: Start writing! Set the pace and write a minimum number of pages each day. Include Contents, Introduction, Acknowledgements, Appendixes, Conclusion, Bibliography & Index. Of course, if you are promoting a Web site, be sure to include plenty of information about it, and give your readers a reason to visit your Web site.

- Editing: Set page size, paginate, apply header and footer, correct misspellings and grammar, arrange your chapters, sections, pace, and visual elements, references, test all hyperlinks, and proofread your manuscript. Since it is well known that our eyes tend to "fill-in" information after we have seen many times, it is always advisable to hire a good editor to polish your masterpiece before publishing.

- Page Setting and Presentation: Apply an international standard book number (ISBN), imprint cover and back cover, write the back page text.

- Finishing and Publishing: Flap details if hardback, send to printer/publisher. Try www.cafepress.com, www.lulu.com or www.booksurge.com. Review sample copy, make any further revisions and send copies to libraries. Assign a national library reference number, and finally, sign-off for publication.

Book Marketing Process

- Reviews – Acquire reviews of the book
- Press kit – Prepare press kit with poster, bookmarks, marketing sheet, sales case, author bio, samples cards etc.
- Web site and Internet – Reserve a Web address and develop a Web site or landing page to market the book. Promote the page using pay-per-click, affiliation, an eBay shop, etc.
- Interviews – Call your local radio stations and newspapers and try and interest them on featuring your book or an interview with the author in their publication or programming. Look for an angle that makes for an interesting story.
- Advertising campaign – Launch an ad campaign depending on your budget. Focus on a medium(s) that your target market will be exposed to the most.
- Bookstore promotion - visit local bookstores and negotiate a sale or return deal or better.
- Book signing – Arrange book signings at bookstores that hold your title.
- Non-bookstore promotion – Read Brian Jud's "Beyond the Bookstore," ISBN: 1-59429-002-4.
- Finding new markets – Re-evaluate your book title and try and see how you can create a new product from it to appeal to a different market, i.e., Talking book, eBook, training course, seminars/webinars, DVD etc. Visit book fairs and talk to people in the industry, promote your book and network.

Resources for Site Promotion Through a Book
http://booksgoogle.com
https://www.lightningsource.com
www.bl.uk/copyright#submission
www.bookmarketingworks.com
www.booksellers.org.uk/events/events_diary.aspr
www.booksurge.com
www.cafepress.com
www.copyrightgov/circs/circ1.html
www.isbn.nielsenbookdata.co.uk
www.isbn-international.org/index.html
www.londonbookfair.co.uk
www.lulu.com
www.plr.uk.com

Table 8: Resources for Web Site Promotion Through a Book

Audio Book

An audio book is a book in audio form. Visit www.audible.com to get a copy of an audio book. Studying professionally produced audio books will show you several things. First, compared to other mediums we have explored so far, it is less effective for marketing your Web site. To produce an audio book you need a microphone, a quiet environment or sound proof booth, audio recording equipment or software, a manuscript of your book and software to convert the sound into MP3.

You can market the audio book through these sites which offer software for creating audio books: www.amazon.com, www.audible.com and www.audiobook creator.com. You can also create an audio book with any sound recording software that is capable of converting files into MP3 format. Once your file is ready, you upload it to your audio book retailer. *See page* 88 on podcasting and *see page* 143 on e-books for more details and links.

Make sure you are in a happy mood and smiling before you read and record your audio book. Record short paragraphs or pages and join them together. Reading longer sections would be more frustrating if you made a mistake. Alternatively you could read long sections and go back and cut out mistakes and re-record just that section to insert in place of the removed section.

If your budget allows, you can turn to professional studios or companies such as www.loftusproductions.co.uk for professional assistance. Search for "audio recording studio [your town]", on the country specific version of a major search engine.

Just like the e-book and books, you should mention your Web site address many times throughout the audio recording. If possible, include your Web site within your audio book title and introduction as well as in the ending.

Newspapers & Magazines

The details covered for e-zines apply to this medium however, in the case of newspapers or magazines a physical product is required to be delivered to customers and potential clients. The cost of production and distribution (including assignment of identification numbers, barcode and registration with various libraries), as well as logistic considerations for the transportation, storage, insurance, delivery and feedback, need close attention. Coupon type cutoff pages or inserts could be used for the feedback questionnaires or application for subscription, etc.

The larger the volume to be produced of the magazine, the more a low cost printer, warehouse storage, insurance and distributer needs to be looked at. A print on demand service such as that offered by www.lulu.com or www.lightning source.com should be considered. To reduce this cost further you may want to consider outsourcing the work to China or India. Companies such as www.rakeshpress.com offer low cost printing at costs that European and American printers just cannot compete with.

For smaller batches, you could consider small runs printed by local printers. However you choose to solve the printing, storage, delivery and insurance challenge, make sure it leaves you with reliable, quality printed material.

With print on demand printers, you only need to pay for small batches or individual prints. This can be one of the lowest short term cost models for printing your newspaper or magazine.

If you are not printing the newspapers or magazine yourself (highly recommended), your other choice is to advertise in a newspaper or magazine or write articles to be included in a newspaper or magazine. This requires you to approach newspapers or magazines that your target customer reads, and asking the editors or editorial support staff to consider either doing a "piece" on your Web site, including an article you have written, or allowing you to advertise your Web site with their newspaper or magazine.

The latter is the most likely to be successful, however, do not neglect the former two. They give you more control and help cut your costs. If selected, you could actually be paid for your article rather than you paying for advertising. You can choose to outsource the article writing to a freelance writer (try www.ifreelance.com or www.guru.com), or write your own.

Writing an Article for Newspaper & Magazine

Newspapers and magazines are read by almost everyone in the Western world. For this reason they charge a handsome sum for advertising, yet a well placed advertisement campaign in a well circulated newspaper or magazine can give you immediate sales, brand awareness and Web site hits. Just like the e-zine or blogs, you can get more results if you are actually featured in the newspaper or magazine, rather than simply placing an advertisement in the medium.

How can you first create newsworthy articles and secondly have them featured in magazines and newspapers that relate to your Web site? We shall discuss this briefly in this section.

Research

- Whenever possible find out from the editors what they are looking for. If you can get the exact requirement of a story, it saves you a lot of time and rejections when you are submitting your article afterwards. If you are unable to get directions or requirements from an editor, study the paper or magazines current and previous articles relating to your Web site content, then draw a template of what is common in all the past articles.

- Now research the topic: get all supporting facts and details. You can use the Internet, industry sources, such as periodicals and other companies in the industry who are prepared to talk to you. Get some quotes and pictures wherever possible.

Writing the Article

- Always use a template whenever you create your articles. It makes it easier to be consistent and professional.

- Theme your article to look like the newspaper's or magazine's articles.

- Always write your headline in the present tense and make it catchy, but accurate. In the last century the limits of accuracy have been pushed beyond the point of breaking by many journalists. Unless the paper or magazine requires it, steer away from such excesses.

- Keep the first sentence short, dramatic and surprising. Use a question or something unexpected as the articles' opening sentence.

- Put the facts first and be clear. Write it in a way which is interesting and refreshing. Try to approach the story from a relatable and human point of view. It is always best to start an article by making the reader visualize a situation, person or event. Readers will be more interested in facts relayed in this manner, rather than simply giving them data.

- In the first paragraph, answer the five W's:

    1) What is the article talking about?
    2) When did the story in the article occur?
    3) Where did the story in the article occur?
    4) Who is the article talking about?
    5) Why did the story in the article occur?

- Throughout your story, be accurate with your facts and figures; however, inject interest through your style of writing.

- After the first paragraph you are ready to give the details of the story. Include several quotes in each article from people you interviewed. Refer to them in the third person, i.e., "he," "she," "it" or "they". Write objectively, using action verbs to give the story a feel of it happening *now*.

- Compose your writing to be fair to each side in the story, and try to present the details in an unbiased manner so that readers can make up their own minds. In some cases a biased article may be requested by the editor- if so, you must do as requested.

- Be creative in how you describe the familiar; avoid clichés and staid statements that bore the reader. If the topic is complicated, simplify it so the reader can easily relate and understand. Write in a sharp, observant manner with attention to detail.

- Whenever appropriate, and in line and supportive of the story, plug your Web site, product or service.

- Find some angle to make the story different.

- In the last paragraph, round the article off. End with a poignant quote or a catchy phrase.

Finalizing the Article

- State that the article is by you and make sure to include your Web site details.

- Now you can look over the format of the article and the layout and decide on where to place images, illustrations and photos. All photos and illustrations must have a caption.

Editing and Correcting the Article

- Spell-check the article. Today, every major word processor or desktop publishing software such as Microsoft Word or Microsoft Publisher comes with grammar and spell checking features – use them.

- Get a friend or colleague or a professional proofreader to proofread your article, looking for grammar, spelling and content errors such as misquotes, false information, inconsistent tone and pacing, etc.

Most of the time editors will edit out your plug; however, they should never remove your by-line; the line at the end containing your name, company and Web site address.

If you need help writing your article search for "professional writers" or place your writing project on www.guru.com or www.ifreelance.com. For a quick free lesson in writing, visit http://designsensory.com/pws. If you are more serious, search for a writing course in your area, e.g., "professional writing courses [your town or city]". For help using a Microsoft word processor, visit:

http://support.microsoft.com/gp/officehub/en-gb.

You do not have to limit yourself to writing articles only for newspapers or magazines. You could write for other mediums also, such as Web sites, news sites, blogs, etc. See the following sites for places to submit your articles:

- http://ezinearticles.com
- www.articleblotter.com
- www.articlecity.com

- www.articlegeek.comg
- www.articlehub.net
- www.articlesbase.com/submit-articles.php
- www.articlesbasecamp.com
- www.e-articles.info
- www.goarticles.com
- www.submityourarticle.com
- www.uniquearticlewizard.com

DVDs

Digital Video Disk (DVD) has all but replaced VHS video tapes. Today, due to their low price and superior storage capacity, they are also threatening to make CDROMs obsolete. Certainly for video, DVDs reign supreme as the portable medium. If you have a course, a recorded webinar, vlog or other digital medium we have already discussed (which can be copied and used as a stand-alone), then DVD may be for you.

You could hand it out at seminars, give it away with your book, use it as a marketing tool to promote your Web site by giving away software, e-books, videos or images – all promoting your Web site.

Make sure the DVD is labeled with a colorful or vivid image or graphic. Include your Web site address clearly on the cover and the actual disk. Make the disk autorun, displaying a splash screen with your Web site details clearly shown. If possible, load your Web site on the computer too. Include sound if your budget allows. Visit the following sites for help with creating a DVD:

- www.apple.com/findouthow/movies
- www.videohelp.com/guides
- Search for "DVD duplication [your city or town]" on any major search engine.

Presentations and Workshops

We have looked at online courses, seminars and other presentations such as vlogs and podcasts. Now we shall turn our attention to speaking mediums.

Live Conferences and Seminars

We have already covered webinars and explored how to create a Web-based seminar, setup a presentation, deliver it and field questions. In a seminar, you stand in front of the audience. There is no digital divide You literally stand in front of your audience and make your presentation.

The process is identical to the webinar. Except for where you would include more slides and images with the webinar; you should rely more on yourself to present the seminar, rather than your visuals and supporting materials. You should use the bare minimum of slides and distracting supporting material, if you can explain this yourself.

You must also limit your attendees to the health and safety restrictions of the venue. Therefore, your seminar will probably be ticketed or offered at a first come first served basis. You will need a lot more supporting staff than with a webinar. You will need assistants to hand out supporting material, a door person, ticket staff, catering staff (if you are offering refreshments) and other supporting staff for audio, visual and lighting.

The cost of seminars is therefore almost always higher than that of a webinar. Make sure your budget will stretch. Evaluate whether the benefits are worth the price.

Presenting at a conference is not the only way you can promote your Web site at these venues; you can also promote your Web site with a stand or booth at a conference. Research to find what conferences are suitable for promoting your Web site. Contact the venue or the conference management, secure a stand and obtain any rules of presenting yourself.

Next, contact your printer, stationer or supplier to acquire posters, a banner, business cards, products, brochures and multimedia devices such as; a screen, computer or DVD player to play your promotional video or demonstration.

The night before the conference, double check that you have packed everything you will need. On the day of the conference, get to the venue early and set up your stand. Test your multimedia equipment, maximize the lighting and arrange the props for maximum effect.

Run a raffle, a poll or some other device that will get visitors to sign up with their names, addresses, phone numbers and e-mail addresses. You could give away your products or offer your service free of charge to the winner. If your products are not appealing in that way, then bring something that is, and offer to give that away to the raffle winner.

If it is within your budget, you could give away prizes throughout the entire day, causing large crowds to gather around your stand frequently, or during every prize draw. If your budget does not allow numerous give-aways, set a time near the end of the conference to draw the winning raffle ticket(s), or select the winner of the competition.

As people start to enter and during the entire day, don't be shy, talk to passersby, engage them in conversation and draw them to your stand. If you have a trial set up, demonstrate it; allow the visitors to sample or try out your product. If you offer a service and not a product, give them a brochure, DVD or something to take away to remember your stand and Web site by. Aim to collect an e-mail address and contact details from every interested visitor. The following are links to conference venues:

- www.allconferences.com
- www.conferences-uk.org.uk
- www.conferencevenues.org

Conferences can be a great place to visit and network to meet people who might be interested in collaborating or doing business with you. In this case, you can use conferences to promote your business, Web site, service or product to other businesses.

Retreats and Workshops

Depending on your business, customer or clients and Web site content, you could arrange a retreat or a workshop. This is ideal for alternative medicine, wine tasting, sports, foreign language learning and most other creative skills, businesses and Web sites.

You can arrange the retreat or workshop as part of a promotion to make people aware of your services and products. Depending on the industry of your Web site, you could actually make money from this retreat or workshop by selling tickets.

There are risks involved with arranging retreats; these are normally related to insurance, in particular, insurance protection for you against any of the retreat or workshop attendees suffering ill health. Make sure you are sufficiently covered and everyone signs a legal contract freeing you from risks not directly connected to you.

During the retreat, remember you are not on vacation. You should be working to make sure everyone of the attendees has a fantastic time and gets to see, try and experience the benefits of your service or product. All supporting material you hand out should have your Web site address and name emblazoned upon it.

Speeches

Giving speeches, like seminars and webinars can be used to promote your business, Web site, product or service. See the webinar section on page 149 for details on organizing your speech. You might wish to make it less formal than the webinar and seminar presentations; however the research, preparation and presentation will be the same.

Inject humor and humility into your speech; aim to keep it short and as informal as is appropriate for the audience. At the end, you do not need to summarize what you have covered in the formal manner of the webinar and seminar.

Similarly the Q&A session should probably be cut from your speech; however, there may be an informal Q&A session after the speech as you meet the guests and audience. Take every opportunity to promote your Web site and business.

Continuity Programs

If you could arrange with your customers so that every month they automatically paid you for your service or a product, wouldn't you be interested? That is exactly what a continuity program does for you. It automatically ships or renews a service contract periodically after billing your customers for it through some form of direct debit or credit card debit instruction.

This system is increasing in popularity with electronic direct response marketers. Continuity programs allow you to sell to the customer once, yet be paid monthly, sometimes indefinitely in the case of a magazine subscription or similar product.

Do not confuse continuity programs with multiple payment plans or hired purchases. With hired purchases you are spreading the cost of a single product. Continuity programs do not do this; they ship a new product every month, and you are paid for this new product every month.

Continuity programs are effective when used for any repeat purchase products or services: such as groceries, magazines, window cleaner, etc. A smart window cleaner who doesn't want to chase his money every month could sign his customers onto a continuity program where he cleans their windows each month, and the client's credit card is debited monthly for the service. In this way the cleaner made the sale once and now can earn the benefits indefinitely.

Motivational material, newsletters, tipster services, diet and fitness or exercise programs, and many other monthly instructional materials are increasingly being sold through this medium.

Review your services and products and see if you can benefit from this type of program. A word of warning concerning abuse of this type of service; Trade Commissions and other consumer watch dogs are gunning for anyone misspelling, misrepresenting, or in anyway deceiving or taking advantage of consumers using continuity programs.

The following are guidelines that should help you steer away from trouble while employing continuity programs:

- Consumers must have a clear understanding of their rights and obligations before they enter into a continuity program contract or agreement.
- The consumer must also express their consent in writing, to enter into such a program.
- Before signing up to a continuity program you must explain to the consumer exactly what they will be receiving, how frequently, what the delivery will contain, the billing procedure, minimum number of purchases (if it applies), and the terms and conditions under which the program may be cancelled. This should all be in writing.
- The consumer must be offered a simple way of cancelling the service.
- If they choose to cancel, upon receipt of the cancellation request, send an acknowledgement of receipt and cease shipping products or providing services and debiting the consumer account.
- If the sale is through a leaflet, catalogue or Web site, the terms and conditions must be clearly displayed next to the sales section, or on the sales page.
- No matter how the consumer arrives at the point of sale (by phone, Web site, in person to the shop, etc.), they must be told of, and given the terms and conditions before the sale commences.
- If you are using telemarketing or some other call center service, you must build this procedure and compliance rules into the script of your sales staff.
- There must be a way of proving that the marketer provides these details to the consumer.
- If radio, television, or other mediums are used, the consumer must be informed via a prominent superscript and a bold text on-screen message, or a loud and clear voiceover informing them that the purchase will use a continuity program.
- A voice over recitation during the sales presentation must also accompany the advertisement to inform the consumer of the payment system to be employed.

- For more details visit the www.ftc.gov/bcp or www.tradingstandards.gov.uk, if you are neither in the UK or U.S., search for "trading standards" or "consumer protection" for your country.

Include free catalogues, leaflets and CD/DVDs that promote your business, service, other products and Web site, in the packaging you send the consumer's products in each month. If you send e-mail confirmation each month, add promotional text links and a banner promoting your Web site, always include an Addthis.com social bookmarking link. The following links lead to continuity programs services suppliers:

- www.continuityprograms.net
- www.drtvfulfillment.com

Conventional Advertising

We shall now briefly look at your conventional marketing options, being: billboards, posters, press releases, public places, radio, television and vehicle wrapping. It has to be said that the price of these mediums can be dramatically higher than that of the online mediums.

Outdoor Marketing

When your budget fits and you want to advertise on a grand scale; locally, nationally or internationally, you can consider using outdoor marketing media such as billboards, building wraps, vehicle wraps, posters, inflatable or airborne advertising.

In many cases, advertising in these formats can be cheaper than television advertising, however, this form of advertising is not suitable for every application and may not always reach your target audience. However, when it does, it is a formidable means of brand awareness and product and/or service promotion.

Today, digital printing processes are used; however, other printing options such as silk screen printing may also be cost effective and viable depending of the requirements. Without going into too much depth concerning the various technologies available, we will briefly analyze the different types of mediums available for outdoor marketing.

Grand Format Digital Printing

Grand format digital printing allows for digital printing of full color images up to 600 dpi or better resolution images, across large surfaces (up to and beyond 126 inches). Larger images are created by tiling smaller images, allowing entire buildings and large surfaces to be wrapped in advertising This solution is great for the following applications:

- Client communications
- Corporate branding
- Directional information
- Employee training
- Location awareness
- Product displays
- Product launches
- Promotional advertising
- Statistical data

The format is also cost effective, allows for fast turnaround as it is printed on demand. To prepare a file for digital printing is easy and the substrate options are numerous. Normally this printing uses six color printing process and can achieve 600 dpi or better. The following are some applications of digital printing:

- Adhesive-backed vinyl decals (*See* vehicle wrapping)
- Awnings
- Backlit signs
- Billboards and posters
- Building wraps
- Carpet messages
- Directional signs
- Electroluminescent signs
- Fencing signs
- Flags
- Freestanding signs
- Murals/wallpaper

- Speaker scrim for stages
- Tents
- Transit signage
- Transparent window clings
- Wallscapes

Search in www.yell.com or through your local business telephone directory for digital printers. Make sure your Web site address is clearly marked on all advertising material no matter the medium you choose. The following are links to Web sites that provide digital printing services:

- www.adamsoutdoor.com
- www.bigskybanners.com
- www.mw-impact.com
- www.outdoorplus.co.uk
- www.postersonwheels.com
- www.roadmedia.co.uk
- www.windship.com

Inflatables and Airborne

Having your brand or advertisement on an inflatable can be another option. Inflatables offer you ease of use, cost efficiency, low maintenance, continuous exposure, easy shipping and storage and it increases brand and location awareness.

Inflatables are great for promoting a product or service, however, with a little creativity you can apply them to many other uses including promoting your Web site. Typically, inflatables would be used for the following uses:

- Brand launches
- Charity events
- Concerts
- Event promotions
- Grand openings
- Parades & fairs
- Point of purchase
- Retail displays
- Sports events

- Tradeshows

Airborne advertisements can be via airships and hot air balloons or blimps, aerial banners and billboard towing. They offer maximum exposure in the sky. Anyone able to see the sky will see them. They use large, easily recognizable lettering, images and branding. They are not normally used at night for obvious reasons. A florescent or illuminated dragged banner could be employed, although it would be rare. There are many options to select from. The following are some of these:

1. Animals
2. Arches
3. Balloons
4. Cell phones
5. Characters
6. Domes
7. Helium inflatables
8. Inflatable-in-a-bag
9. Inflate-a-sign
10. Kiosks
11. Logos
12. Objects
13. Podiums
14. Projection screen
15. Sealed minis
16. Sports cages
17. Tents
18. Truck bed inflatable billboard
19. Tunnels
20. Vehicles
21. Walkabout® costumes
22. Wind Dancers® (E.G., air flames, characters, fly guys, shorties, sky ticklers, vertitubes).

Search for "aerial advertising" or "balloon advertising" on any major search engine. Here are a few examples of what you will find:

- http://skyads.uk.net
- www.aerialbanners.com
- www.aerialservices.org
- www.airads.co.uk
- www.airadvertising.co.uk
- www.airsign.com
- www.ballooning.fsnet.co.uk
- www.gasserbanners.com
- www.giantadvertisingblimps.com
- www.skyvertising.com
- www.skywrite.com
- www.towplanes.com
- www.usairads.com

The following is a list of companies that offer inflatable advertising services. Search for "inflatable advertising" on any major search engine for local suppliers:

- www.airadpromotions.com
- www.windship.com/HPI_inflatable_advertising.asp

Vehicle Wrapping

Vehicles are everywhere nowadays and international vehicle ownership trends are on the rise, most especially in China, India and Brazil. The surface area of vehicles offers a great opportunity for advertising. With a colorful, attractive design, a wrapped vehicle travelling through a busy city will get noticed by thousands of people a day. Even on the freeways and urban areas, a brightly wrapped vehicle stands out and its advertising message will generally be remembered. Vehicle wrapping can be done through the following methods:

1. Airbrushing/spraying
2. Decals – adhesive backed
3. Magnetic
4. Window film
5. Wraps

The vehicle wrapping industry is growing with many fleet owners employing the medium to offer advertising on their trucks, trailers and caravans, trains, boats, ships, planes, helicopters and roadside stalls. You can also benefit from this effective medium. The following sites specialize in vehicle wrapping:

- http://epicmediagroup.com
- http://realwraps.com
- www.adsgonemobile.com
- www.ad-wraps.com
- www.autocarwraps.com/home.html
- www.buswraps.com
- www.carwrap.com
- www.carwraps.net
- www.carwrapusa.com
- www.covereduk.co.uk
- www.gatorwraps.com
- www.inchmere-design.com
- www.pyramidvisuals.co.uk/services/vehicle_wrap
- www.signheredigital.com
- www.signsexpress.co.uk/productsVehicle.cfm
- www.skinzwraps.com
- www.windship.com/HPDV_vehicle.asp
- www.wrapvehicles.com

You can also search for "car wrapping" or "vehicle wraps" on any major search engine to find more information or resources from which to choose.

If you employ this medium (investigate wrapping or decaling your own vehicle with your company name, logo and Web site address), you should make sure the design is highly attractive, interesting and effective as a marketing tool. Place your Web site name somewhere prominent and consider having the design on the back as well as the sides of your vehicle. Spend money where it will be noticed, therefore avoid decaling roofs and other less visible parts of the vehicle.

Public Advertising Places

If you own office Real Estate in a prominent location, i.e., center of a city or next to a busy road or freeway, you could opt to wrap the building with your brand, products, Web site details, etc. Over time, this will become a landmark, and your brand or building will be firmly established in the local community.

Utilizing large solvent or ultra violet printers such as those produced by http://gandinnovations.com: grand scale printers can print on polyester, cotton or acrylic hybrid canvass, any design you require. The breathable cloths are ideal for scaffolding and buildings where wind is a consideration. The permeable mesh limits flapping and wind resisting. The following are some companies that supply building wraps:

- www.cestrian.couk
- www.icondisplay.co.uk
- www.podigroup.co.uk
- www.pyramidvisuals.co.uk/services/building_wrap
- www.superchrome.co.uk
- www.usaimage.com
- www.windship.com

Indoor Marketing

There are a host of indoor advertising mediums available to you. Some of them include:

- A-Frames
- Backdrops
- Banners
- Carpets
- Danglers
- Displays
- Floor graphics
- Murals
- Posters
- Table skirts

Whether at an exhibition, busy train station, gallery or shopping mall, indoor advertising creates a buzz, promotes your brand and informs people of where to find you. Budget allowing, be sure to explore this medium also for promoting your company, product, service and Web site.

Press Releases

With every launch, be it for a Web site, product, or service, it is greatly advised that you send out a press release regarding the event. Typically, press releases need to be maximized to make use of timing. There is no need in sending out the press release on the same or next day of the event. Press releases need to be sent out sufficiently ahead of the event to allow their distribution, delivery and digestion by the news network and audience.

The press release is an excellent SEO tool because it can carry your SEO optimized copy written article with your Web site link imbedded in the message to news networks, journalists, social networkers, bloggers and others.

When the release is picked up and displayed on a Web site, e-mail, blog or social networking group, forum, or profile page, a back-link is immediately created to your site. It therefore makes sense that you make your press release as newsworthy as possible so that you increase the number of Web sites that will be interested in featuring it.

We have already gone through article writing, most of the rules and the best practices for article writing apply for press releases also, however a few new ones need to be considered. These are as follows:

> **NOTE:** It is more effective to have your article written by a third party, seemingly unrelated with your Web site or business, rather than writing it yourself.

1) Include your Web site address within the article and if the article was written by you or your staff, also include your Web site address in the author details.

2) Make your article newsworthy and include as much multimedia as possible, i.e., images, video and sound.

3) Tag all your multimedia attachments with title, description, keywords, etc.

4) Tag the actual release with as many relevant release tags as you are allowed by your PR host.

5) Syndicate your press release via RSS.

6) Target industries and geographic locations where your press release is likely to interest the most people.

7) Select release date carefully; make it coincide with an associated event, national holiday or significant date relating to your press release.

8) Use Trackback and Pingback to track your release. These services may be provided by your PR host, if not, change hosts. There is a list of PR hosts at the end of this list.

9) Use relevant keywords in the URL for the press release.

10) Give your press release the look and feel of a print article with highlighted quotes.

11) SEO the press release. Analyze the keyword density of the article to determine if you have included relevant keywords and keyword phrases. Check your competitor's successful press releases and use the Google keyword tool to determine what keywords and keyword phrases to highlight in your press release.

12) Subscribe to a monitoring service for your press release. Normally, this service is offered by your PR host at extra cost. You can track the distribution of your press release and find out what percentage was read, downloaded as e-book, downloaded as PDF file, printed, read via RSS/XML /Atom, e-mail, news networks such as Pheedo Network and Topix Network, etc. Some PR hosts also distribute your release via JavaScript and directly on their own Web site. Statistics for these destinations should also be available. Some PR hosts provide weekly stats, search engine hits stats, and geographically displayed stats (via

points on Google Maps, etc.). All these give you the statistical data to fine-tune your current press release or future releases.

13) Attach social bookmarking links.

The Following are PR hosts:

- http://express-press-release.com
- http://prweb.com
- www.eworldwire.co.uk
- www.massmediadistribution.com
- www.pabusiness.co.uk
- www.pr.com
- www.pressbox.co.uk
- www.pressmethod.com

PR Tracking

- https://secure.cyberalert.com

Search for "PR distribution [your country or region of interest]" or "press release distribution [your country or region of interest]" on any major search engine for local PR distribution firms to you.

Remember your press release is to the press— not the end reader; therefore cater it to appeal to journalists. *See* Writing an Article for Newspaper & Magazine on page 159, www.publicityinsider.com/freesecret.asp, www.nsti.org/press /prtips.html or search for "how to write a press release" on any major search engine for further assistance.

Radio and Television

Radio and television offer strong and formidable mediums for advertising. However, they can be very costly, especially if you waste money advertising to the wrong audience. The statistics on radio and television coverage is impressive; however what the general statistic does not tell you are what percentage of that market is looking for your product or service.

If only you could get that much precision in your market research. Alas, you cannot. You have to make do with the statistics and demographic sales information from the radio stations and television stations/networks.

In this section we tackle how to advertise and use television and radio to promote your Web site. We shall start off with using the mediums and end in advertising details.

Free TV or Radio Promotion for Your Web Site

Few Web site launches are newsworthy enough for an interview to be requested by a TV or Radio station. However, a product, service or the personal life of the Web site owner or an associate may be interesting news to TV and radio stations.

When looking to utilize radio and TV stations, first seek to do so free of charge before you seek to pay. There are a few advantages and disadvantages to free TV and radio publicity. These are as follows:

Advantages
- It is free and therefore saves you a fortune in advertising fees.

Disadvantages
- You do not control the programming – the snippet/story/program may not be aired at the most effective time for reaching your target audience.
- You do not control the angle on the story – the journalist or station may decide to use the story in a way that negatively affects your Web site traffic.
- You do not control the frequency in which the story is aired.

With all the disadvantages aside, there is a saying that may or may not be true, "any publicity is good publicity". I would like to change that to "any free publicity is good publicity".

To get free publicity, you have to do something that is newsworthy in the eyes of radio and TV stations. The larger networks become, there are so many stories that are trying to compete with them, that it will be more difficult than aiming for a softer target, such as smaller stations.

There are many small towns and Internet radio stations that are vying endlessly for local or interesting news. With them, your news, story, product or service may stand more of a chance of being headlined. Similarly, cable TV channels and small networks also love to receive newsworthy local news.

Approach these smaller stations first, before you head for CNN, Reuters, Bloomberg, ABC, BBC, ITV, and SKY networks. Next, contact the stations' news program manager and inquire if the station will be interested in your story. The following is a small list of some of these stations:

Radio	Television
http://music.aol.com/radio guide/full-radio-station-list-a	http://archive.museophile.org/ broadcast
http://radio-mall.com/radiomal.htm	www.galaxy-marketing.com/channel_list.htm
www.digitalradionow.com /statl.php	www.ionmedia.tv/stations
www.listenlive.eu/uk.html	www.nettvdb.com
www.londoncreative.com	www.newsdirectory.com/tv.php
www.mediauk.com/radio/ starting-with	www.newsdirectory.com/tv.php?network=1
www.rab.co.uk	www.sbgi.net/business/television.shtml
www.radioadvertising.org .uk	www.stationindex.com/tv/tv-markets
www.radiofeeds.co.uk	www.stationindex.com/tv/tv-markets-100
www.radiorepublic.co.uk	www.webtvlist.com
www.radioworks.co.uk	

TABLE 9: Radio and Television Marketing Resources

Paying for TV and Radio Advertising

To make the best use of the list of radio and TV stations, you need to understand exactly how you need to approach your paid radio or TV marketing campaign. The following are pointers on how to do this:

- **Research:** Write down exactly what your Web site is offering, and what type of audience you need to reach. Remember, you are trying to get the best audience for your money; therefore think about who will be paying for your service or product, not necessarily who will be using it. One example of an innovative, new television advertising company offering reduced priced advertising is www.spotrunner.com.

- **Profile:** Build a profile of your target market. Include sex, age, educational level, geographic area, ethnic group, number of children in the home, children's ages and other specialist topics like credit card owner, vacation preference, car type, favorite TV shows, current cell phone payment package, etc. Also include information on what the profile audience is interested in from the radio or TV station. For example, a Real Estate agent would be interested to know about people who are looking to buy or sell their houses, and possibly programming serving his/her topic of interest.

- **Match:** Call the sales rep. of the radio or TV station and arrange to send or meet with him/her, to discuss how their program audiences match your profile. If there is a match, the rep. should be able to give you figures and statistic for viewers, programs, times, costs, etc., that will best serve your profile requirements. Program timings, ratings breakdown, signal coverage maps and package costs can be supplied by the sales rep. of any fairly well organized radio or TV station.

- **The Package**: Make sure you understand the average number of people that will hear your advertisement in an hour, day or week, etc., and how much it will cost to reach 1% of your target audience population: also known as CPP (cost-per-point).

- **Sponsorship**: You can choose to sponsor news or a program that will be seen and/or heard by your target audience. This is a great way to make sure your brand, Web site address, product or service is promoted every time the show is aired and often before and after advertisement breaks. Ask your ad. sales rep. about "pre-roll spots".

- **Local Community and Special Events:** Some TV and radio stations, especially local stations, offer other opportunities of special mentions. Look for local events and other special events that you can allign your brand/service with. Your service or brand will get a mention during announcements for the event. Make sure you focus specifically on events that are well attended by your target audience. For television, make sure you have a visual representation of your Web site, e.g., a T-shirt with your logo and site address, or a cap or hat, etc.

- **Create the Spot or Ad:** This is a specialist area and I advise you to look for a local agent or agency who can help supply the talent to execute an effective radio or TV advertisement. Remember, whatever you do will be associated with your Web site, brand, product or service for a long time. Therefore, make it look as you would like your Web site to be thought of, (professional, honest and reliable – I hope).

- **The Ad or Spot**: Great ads and radio spots tend to use humor and emotion, sex or a mixture of all these. By sex I do not mean literally. I am referring to the use of provocative, titillating and suggestive images, scenes or speech. Compelling music and sounds, funny scenes, unusual voices and conversations that tell a relatable story to your target audience, is probably what you should aim for. If your advertisement is part of a long advertisement campaign, create a story with different ads that tell parts of the story. This allows you to maintain interest in your ads through long periods.

- **Contact:** Always include in your advertisement or spot, a memorable or easily remembered URL and/or phone number. Use the same URL and/or phone number with all ads in the campaign.

- **Source Production:** Contact the TV or radio station and ask the sales rep. what production company the station recommends. This will most likely save you a lot of time and trouble. However a quick search on any major search engine for "radio spot production [your town, city, or country]", "radio commercials production [your town, city, or country]", or "TV commercials production [your town, city, or country]" will yield a list of your local production companies.

- **Manage Production:** Work with the production company and come up with a script. Agree on a schedule, milestones and deadlines. If possible, build in penalties (they forfeit part of their payment) for delays or missed deadlines. Monitor them closely without getting in their way.

Search Engine Optimization

Conclusion

Conclusion

The Internet today has invaded our entire lives and is quickly overtaking many conventional forms of doing business. Many people now own Web sites but are finding that simply owning a Web site is not enough to be successful in the new Internet world. Today, you need to make sure you are found by the users of the Internet.

In the domain of the searcher, the search engine reigns supreme. This industry has created Google, Microsoft Live, Yahoo! (who might be taken over by Microsoft in the near future), AOL and many others. These search engines are sophisticated, money making enterprises whose currency is traffic. To buy into this search economy you have to get some of that traffic to your Web site.

This book has been an effort to compile as much information about making your Web site rank high on search engines through the use of META tags, domain name registration, search engine submissions, directory submissions and foreign language support.

After covering all this in chapter two, we headed for the new school of Web marketing and social marketing. Social networking sites today dominate the traffic wars on the Internet. With millions each day joining networks, sharing ideas, experiences, images, videos and stories, these Internet social networks are proving a formidable tool for sales and marketing.

We covered Wikis, social networking sites, social bookmarking, forums, groups, blogs, vlogs, mo-blogs, photo-blogs, bittorrent, peer-to-peer networks and podcasting. The wealth of multimedia technology available today is opening up new avenues for Web masters, marketers and SEO specialists to drive traffic to the sites they promote.

In chapter four, we turned our attention towards sales. It is great driving traffic; however, will that traffic necessarily buy from your site? The answer is "no", you have to drive the right traffic to increase your sales conversions. We started with free methods of promoting and improving sales on your Web site.

With Google and Yahoo! Internet Marketing dwarfing the Internet market, we didn't have to look far for the most effective tools in use today. We looked first at the Yahoo! Internet Marketing's offering of pay-per-click, paid directory listing, and local listings. Next, we examined affiliations, and affiliate marketing, eBay and e-mail marketing ending with a warning against spam and abusive usage of e-mail addresses.

Chapter five was solely dedicated to Google and their AdWords and Analytical services. We examined how these tools could be used to analyze traffic metrics; and based on the findings, you could fine-tune your Web site to increase conversions.

The sixth chapter was dedicated to online and conventional ways of promoting your Web site. We tackled the online mediums, first looking at e-courses, e-books, e-zines, and webinars.

Not to be under estimated, conventional, offline mediums such as books, audio books, newspapers and magazines, DVDs, live conferences and workshops were also discussed.

We looked at advertising with posters, billboards, inflatables and aerial advertising. With digital printing now able to produce printed canvasses that can be used to literally wrap entire buildings, conventional advertising has never had it so good. We also explored other types of advertizing such as vehicle wrapping and indoor advertising mediums.

Before ending chapter six we looked at radio and television, and examined how these two medium could be used for free, and also by paying for placements.

I hope you have enjoyed and found this book informative, and that it has given you many new ideas on how to promote your Web site. A large part of SEO is iterative and so you cannot expect to get 100% results from a single sitting, however, if you dedicate a small amount of your time to it daily, you will yield incredible results and greatly improve your conversion rate, hit rate and return on investment.

Search Engine Optimization

Appendices

Appendix 1 Social Networking Sites

General Social Networking	
NAME	**WEB SITE**
Bebo	www.bebo.com
Buzznet	www.buzznet.com
Care2	www.care2.com
Cyworld	www.cyworld.com
eSPIN-the-Bottle	www.espinthebottle.com
FaceBook	www.facebook.com
FaceParty	www.faceparty.com
Hi5	www.hi5.com
IMEEM	http://photoswww.imeem.com
Mashable	www.mashable.com
Meetup (Local meet-ups, clubs and groups).	www.meetup.com
Multiply	http://multiply.com
MySpace	www.myspace.com
Netlog	http://netlog.com
Piczo	www.piczo.com
ProfileHeaven	www.profileheaven.com
StumbleUpon	www.stumbleupon.com
TagWorld	www.tagworld.com
Twitter	www.twitter.com

General Social Networking	
NAME	**WEB SITE**
WAYN	www.wayn.com
Xanga	www.xanga.com
Yahoo! 360° (Yahoo! owned).	http://360.yahoo.com

Niche Social Networking		
NAME	**DESCRIPTION**	**WEB SITE**
Adult Only	Friend finder sites.	www.adultfriendfinder.com & www.alt.com
BlackPlanet	African American community.	www.blackplanet.com
CarDomain	Various vehicles.	www.cardomain.com
Dodgeball	Mobile social software.	www.dodgeball.com
Flickr	Photo sharing.	www.flickr.com
Gaia Online	Multi-player role-playing games.	www.gaiaonline.com
Joga	Soccer genre; Nike owned.	www.joga.com
Last.fm	Music community.	www.last.fm
LinkedIn	Business field.	www.linkedin.com
LiveJournal	General sharing.	www.livejournal.com
PlayAhead	UK teenage genre.	www.playahead.co.uk
SoundPedia	Music community.	http://soundpedia.com
XING	Professional.	www.xing.com
XuQa	Poker.	http://xuqa.com

Foreign Language Social Networking		
NAME	**DESCRIPTION**	**WEB SITE**
Grono	Polish	http://grono.net
Hyves	Dutch- six languages.	www.hyves.nl
IWiW	Hungarian	http://iwiw.hu
LunarStorm	Swedish	www.lunarstorm.se
MiGente	Latino	www.migente.com
Mixi	Japanese	www.mixi.jp
Passado	Italiano, Français, Deutsch, Español, English	http://uk.wasabi.com
PlayAhead	Swedish Teenagers	www.playahead.se

Reunion Social Networking School, College & University	
NAME	WEB SITE
Classmates	www.classmates.com
Friends Reunited	www.friendsreunited.com
Graduates.com	http://graduates.com
MyYearbook	www.myyearbook.com
Reunion.com	www.reunion.com
Student Center, The (Latin Students)	www.student.com

Appendix 2 Foreign Language Search Engine Listing

COUNTRY	DESCRIPTION	WEB SITE
	Foreign Language Search Engine Listing Sites	
Canada:	Bellzinc.ca	http://directory.bellzinc.ca /bellzinc/english/queries/c _reg.asp
	Canada One Business Directory	www.canlinks.net/addalin k
China:	Baidu	http://site.baidu.com
	Google China	www.google.com/dirhp?h l=zh-CN&tab=wd&q=
	MyRice (Owned by Yahoo!)	http://search.myrice.com/ dir.htm
	Netease	http://dir.so.163.com
	Sina	http://dir.iask.com
	Sogou	http://www.sogou.com/dir
	Tom	http://search.tom.com/dir
	Yasou	http://site.yahoo.com.cn
	Zhongsou	www.zhongsou.com
Germany:	Allesklar (Listings start at 199,00 EUR Annual Renewal)	allesklar.de/listing.php.
	Allesklar (Free Submit)	https://listing.allesklar.de/ mt_shop/mt_basisdesc.ph p
	Bellnet (Free listing or express	http://bellnet.de/suchen/an meldungsseite.html

Foreign Language Search Engine Listing Sites		
COUNTRY	**DESCRIPTION**	**WEB SITE**
	listing-50 EUR).	
Germany: (continued)	ShareLook Deutschland (Free listing or express listing-98 EUR).	www.sharelook.de
	WEB.DE (Listings start at 180 EUR-annual renewal).	http://eintragsservice.web.de
Israel:	Nana	http://index.nana.co.il/addsite/addsite.asp
	ODP - Open Directory Project (To submit to the Israeli directory in English).	www.dmoz.org/Regional/Middle_East/Israel
	ODP - Open Directory Project (Hebrew)	http://dmoz.org.il
	Science	http://science.co.il/contact.asp
	Tapuz	www.tapuz.co.il/index/Index.asp
	Walla	http://buy.walla.co.il/ts.cgi?tsscript=guide/add.site
Switzerland:	AllesKlar (Germany - Free listing or express listing starts at 199,00 EUR-	Search: allesklar.ch Submit: https://listing.allesklar.de/mt_portal.php

Foreign Language Search Engine Listing Sites		
COUNTRY	DESCRIPTION	WEB SITE
	annual renewal).	
	Express Submit	http://manitoo.ch/promotion/inscription_expresse.php
Switzerland: (continued)	Manitoo (Free listing or express listing 50,00 CHF).	Search: manitoo.ch Free Submit: www.manitoo.ch/promotion/inscription_gratuite.php
	ODP – Open Directory Projects	Search: dmoz.org Submit German: www.dmoz.org/World/Deutsch/Regional/Europa/Schweiz Submit French: dmoz.org/World/Français/Régional/Europe/Suisse Submit Italian: www.dmoz.org/World/Italiano/Regionale/Europa/Svizzera
	Sharelook.ch (Free listing or express listing-98,00 EUR). (Choose an appropriate category and click on Neueintrag-left side-Index for Swiss German	Search: sharelook.ch Submit: www.sharelook.ch.

Foreign Language Search Engine Listing Sites		
COUNTRY	**DESCRIPTION**	**WEB SITE**
	Web sites).	
Switzerland: (continued)	Yahoo! (Germany-Free listing in Yahoo!'s European directories-except UK).	Search: www.de.yahoo.com

Appendix 3 Video Sharing Sites

Video Sharing Sites		
NAME	**DESCRIPTION**	**WEB SITE**
4Shared	Free file sharing; 5GB free space.	www.4shared.com
5Show	Asian site.	www.5show.com
AOL	American site.	http://video.aol.com
Badongo	Free file hosting and sharing.	www.badongo.com
BigUpload	File hosting.	www.bigupload.com
Blip.tv	Video shows.	http://blip.tv
Bocoo	Supports capitalization.	www.bocoo.com
Bunkster	East Asian.	www.bunkster.se
CrunchyRoll	Asian "YouTube".	www.crunchyroll.com
DailyMotion	Video uploading.	www.dailymotion.com
DANWEI	Chinese media advertising.	www.danwei.org
FileFactory	Image and video editing/file hosting.	www.filefactory.com/r
FileFront	Games and video	www.filefront.com
FLuRL	Video sharing	www.flurl.com
Google Video	United Kingdom	http://video.google.co.uk
Heavy	General sharing.	www.heavy.com
hi5	Multilingual support.	www.hi5.com
Humyo	Media file storage, access, sending and	www.humyo.com

Video Sharing Sites		
NAME	**DESCRIPTION**	**WEB SITE**
	publishing.	
Hupo	Asian site.	www.hupo.tv
Internet Archive	Non- profit movie, video and television show archives.	www.archive.org/details /movies
JumpCut	Free picture and movie upload, edit and sharing.	www.jumpcut.com
MegaShare	File hosting.	http://megashare.com
Megaupload	Supports capitalization.	www.megaupload.com
MegaVideo	Supports capitalization.	www.megavideo.com
MySpace	Social networking and video sharing.	http://vids.myspace.com
MyVideo	South African.	www.myvideo.co.za
OUOU	East Asian.	www.ouou.com
PhotoBucket	Photo and video sharing.	http://photobucket.com
PutFile	General sharing.	www.putfile.com
RapidShare	100MB max per file hosting.	http://rapidshare.com
RapidUp-Load	Free file and Web hosting.	www.rapidupload.com
Revver	General sharing.	http://revver.com
Sina	Chinese news and culture portal.	www.sina.com

Video Sharing Sites		
NAME	**DESCRIPTION**	**WEB SITE**
Spread-It	File storage and sharing.	www.spread-it.com
Stage6	Video files.	www.stage6.com
SuperNova-Tube	Video uploading.	www.supernovatube.com
TinyPic	Image and video sharing.	http://tinypic.com
Tudou	East Asian.	www.tudou.com
TVix.cn	Chinese file sharing.	TVix.cn
Uploading	File hosting.	www.uploading.com
USA Upload	Large file backup and sending.	www.usaupload.net
UUme	East Asian.	http://uume.com
Vbunk	General sharing.	http://vbunk.com
Veoh	TV and video streaming.	www.veoh.com
Vimeo	Video exchange.	www.vimeo.com
Vsocial	Media sharing.	www.vsocial.com
Yahoo! Video	General sharing.	http://video.yahoo.com
Youku	East Asian.	www.youku.com
youSENDit	Up to 2 GB file sending.	www.yousendit.com
YouTube	General sharing.	www.youtube.com
Zango	Video and games sharing; supports capitalization.	www.zango.com

Video Sharing Sites		
NAME	**DESCRIPTION**	**WEB SITE**
ZippyVideos	Media sharing.	www.zippyvideos.com
zSHARE	File sharing.	http://zshare.net

Appendix 4 Free Vlogging Sites

Free Vlogging Sites
WEB SITE
(HELP): www.node101.org
http://blip.tv
http://freevlog.org
http://mefeedia.com
http://photobucket.com
http://uncutvideo.aol.com/Main.do
http://video.google.com
http://video.msn.com/video.aspx?mkt=en-gb
http://video.yahoo.com
www.blinkx.com
www.crackle.com
www.flixya.com
www.metacafe.com
www.revver.com
www.veoh.com
www.vidblogs.com
www.videocasting-station.com
www.vidlogs.com
www.vimeo.com
www.youtube.com

Appendix 5 Entrepreneurial Vlogging Sites

Entrepreneurial Vlogging Sites	
DESCRIPTION	**WEB SITE**
BUSINESS:	http://adhoc.blinkx.com
	www.thevideosense.com
DIRECTORIES:	http://videoblogging-universe.com/vlogs
	www.01vlog.com
	www.videopodcasts.tv
	www.youcandoitpublishing.com
Opt-in RSS to Mail Subscription:	http://vlogdir.com/service
	www.livevideo.com
Tutorials:	http://community.vlogmap.org

Appendix 6 Polling Sites

Polling Sites	
WEB SITE	**DESCRIPTION**
http://buzzdash.com	Start polls on topics including news, sports, politics to relationships, philosophy and religion or participate in the existing ones.
http://doodle.ch	Create, publish and send polls.
http://freepollkit.com	Insert HTML snippet polls into your existing site.
http://ipoll.surveygizmo.com	Allows iPhone users to create polls.
http://polldaddy.com	Create polls for Web sites, blogs or share by e-mail.
http://pollgenius.com	Create or search existing polls.
http://pollpub.com	Polls for MySpace, blogs and social networks.
http://polls.zoho.com	Create free polls.
http://quibblo.com	Allows users to create and collaborate with others via polls, surveys and content around various topics.
http://rankthese.com	Online rankings, polls, and surveys.
http://rateitall.com	Rate and share opinions.
http://tappity.com	Web site driven by users-allows submission, rating & discovery of mobile-friendly Web pages for display in various mobile devices and phones.
http://twiigs.com	Create polls or vote on them.

Polling Sites	
WEB SITE	**DESCRIPTION**
www.easy-poll.com	Allows multi-colors for your polls and multi-choice answers as well as standard yes/no.
www.embracemobile.com	Market research surveys over cell phones for things such as user opinions, customer satisfaction or brand awareness.
www.feefo.com/feefo	Customer feedback, ratings, opinions, and reports tool.
www.flektor.com	Watch videos, photos, movies & create polls for your social networking profiles. Owned by MySpace - aimed at younger crowd.
www.freepolls.com	Create free polls or pay to make them advertising-free.
www.free-website-polls.com	Up to 20 choices of polls for Web sites & blogs
www.guessnow.com	Predict future events and capitalize on your points.
www.imedialearn.com/imediapoll	Create online polls and control the look-and-feel.
www.micropoll.com	Create, customize, and use polls on your Web site
www.mobiode.com	Create mobile surveys and collect user's mobile data.
www.nexo.com	Share pictures, videos, tasks, polls and comment.
www.pollplaza.nl/pages	Dutch Web site for creating and participating in polls.
www.pollsb.com	Social discussion site.

Polling Sites	
WEB SITE	**DESCRIPTION**
www.pulsepoll.com	Lets you create a poll with and grab some script to paste in your site.
www.quimble.com	Create, vote & search for polls.
www.snappoll.com	Choose colors and layout and prevents multiple votes.
www.sodahead.com	Create and vote on public polls.
www.sonarhq.com	Makes online consultation easy.
www.sportspoll.co.uk	Sports polling.
www.surveypopups.com	Embed poll widget into your site.
www.tezaa.com	User driven community, create, modify and participate in polls.
www.toluna.com	Create and vote on polls free.
www.vizu.com	Create free polls for your blog or engage in targeted marketing research
www.vovici.com/products	Online survey software for individuals to global enterprises.
www.webpasties.com	Add a poll, an RSS ticker or a slideshow on any Web site.

Appendix 7 Traffic Exchange Sites

Traffic Exchange Sites	
NAME	**WEB SITE**
Advertising Knowhow	www.advertisingknowhow.com
All Fresh Clicks	www.allfreshclicks.com
Bionic Hits	http://bionichits.com
Click Thru	www.clickthru.com
Click Voyager	www.clickvoyager.com
Clickin Fingers	http://clickinfingers.com
Clicking Crazy	http://clickingcrazy.biz
ClicksMatrix	www.clicksmatrix.com
Clix Swap	www.clixswap.com
Deep Sea Hits	http://deepseahits.com
Easy Hits4 U	www.easyhits4u.com
Eternal Hits	www.eternalhits.com
Fast Freeway	www.fastfreeway.com
Fontoon	www.fontoon.com
Forever Traffic	www.forevertraffic.com
Funny Farm Traffic	www.funnyfarmtraffic.com
Hit Harvester	www.hitharvester.com
Hit Pulse	www.hitpulse.com
Hit Safari	www.hitsafari.com
Hit Sense	www.hitsense.com
Hit Vortex	www.hitvortex.com
I Love Clicks	www.iloveclicks.com

Traffic Exchange Sites	
NAME	**WEB SITE**
I Love Hits	www.ilovehits.com
Jack Ten Forty	www.jacktenforty.com
Mystical Maze	www.mysticalmaze.com
ProHits Plus	http://prohitsplus.com
Start Xchange	www.startxchange.com
Top Surfer	http://topsurfer.com
Traffic Flare	http://trafficflare.com
Traffic Meet	www.trafficmeet.com
Traffic Pods	www.trafficpods.com
Traffic Roundup	www.trafficroundup.com
Traffic Soldiers	www.trafficsoldiers.com
Traffic Swarm	www.trafficswarm.com
TS25	http://ts25.com
Web Biz Insider	www.webbizinsider.com
WebMaster Quest	www.webmasterquest.com
Wolf Surfer	www.wolfsurfer.com

Appendix 8 Infosite Listings

Infosite Listings	
DESCRIPTION	**WEB SITE**
Books:	http://booksgoogle.com
	http://isbndb.com
	http://onlinebooks.library.upenn.edu
	www.amazon.com
Computer Games:	www.games-db.com
Computer & Internet:	http://kb.iu.edu
	http://kb.mozillazine.org/Knowledge_Base
	http://kbase.info.apple.com
	http://kbase.redhat.com
	http://support.esri.com.
	http://support.microsoft.com
	www.icthubknowledgebase.org.uk
	www.oscommerce.info
Films:	www.imdb.com
Finance:	www.investopedia.com
Government:	https://www.cia.gov/library/publications/the-world-factbook/index.html
	www.hmrc.gov.uk
	www.irs.gov
	www.parliament.uk
	www.usa.gov
Images:	http://images.google.com
	www.fotosearch.com

Infosite Listings	
DESCRIPTION	**WEB SITE**
Legal Education:	www.law.cornell.edu
	www.nolo.com
Maps:	http://maps.google.com
	http://maps.live.com
	www.mapquest.com
Music:	www.allmusic.com
	www.onlinemusicdatabase.com
	www.sing365.com
News Archives:	http://news.google.com

Appendix 9 Free Ad Posting Sites

Free Ad Posting Sites
WEB SITE
http://adsfree.forumwise.com
http://postadsfree.forumwise.com
http://postfreeads.free-forums.org
www.freeadforum.com
www.freeads.biztop.com
www.freeadvertisingboard.com
www.freeadvertisingforum.com
www.postfreeadsforum.com
www.postyouradforfree.com

Appendix 10 Affiliate Programs

Affiliate Programs
WEB SITE
http://affiliate-program.amazon.com/gp/associates/join
http://www.westernunion.com/WUCOMWEB/staticMid.do? method=load&pagename=aboutUsAffiliate
https://chitika.com
www.affiliatecommission.net
www.affiliatefuel.com
www.affiliatefuture.co.uk
www.affiliatemarketing.co.uk
www.affiliatewindow.com
www.amwso.com
www.apple.com/itunes/affiliates
www.cj.com
www.clickbank.com
www.clickxchange.com
www.clixgalore.com
www.linkshare.com
www.microsoftaffiliates.net
www.partnercentric.com
www.performics.com
www.shareasale.com
www.shareresults.com
www.sonystyle.com
www.thomascook.com/content/help/help-lp/affiliates.asp

Affiliate Programs
WEB SITE
www.tradedoubler.com
www.valuecommerce.ne.jp
www.widgetbucks.com
www.xl.com/About_Us/Affiliates.asp

Appendix 11 E-Book Resources

E-Book Resources	
DESCRIPTION	**WEB SITE**
E-Book Conversion:	https://www.mobipocket.com/ebookbase/en/homepage/conversion.asp
E-Book Creation:	www.ebookswriter.com
	www.yudu.com
E-Book Store Creation:	www.amazon.com
	www.cafepress.com
	www.google.com/base
	www.lulu.com
	www.make-a-store.com
E-Book Marketing Help:	www.guidetoebookmarketing.com
Distribution:	http://booksgoogle.com
	www.audiobooksforfree.com
	www.froogle.com
	www.lightningsource.com
	www.mobilebooks.org
Organizations:	http://gutenberg.net.au
	http://ibiblio.org
	http://literalsystems.org/abooks/index.php
	www.gutenberg.cc
	www.librivox.org
	www.worldlibrary.net
Note:	Search for "ebook [creation tools] [publishers] [distribution][store]

E-Book Resources	
DESCRIPTIO N	WEB SITE
[conversion]" on any major search engine.	

Notes

Search Engine Optimization

Bibliography

Blankson, Samuel. 2007. *META Tags: Optimizing Your Web Site for Internet Search Engines.* s.l. : Blankson Enterprises Ltd., 2007.

Bly, Robert W. 1990. *The Copywriter's Handbook, Third Edition: A Step-By-Step Guide To Writing Copy That Sells.* s.l. : Holt Paperbacks; updated edition, 1990.

Gabay, Jonathon. 2007. *Gabay's Copywriters' Compendium-revised edition in paperback: The Definitive Professional Writers Guide.* Burlington, MA : Elsevier Ltd., 2007.

Jud, Brian. *Beyond the Bookstore.*

Index

Printed in the United States
¹22373LV00010B/25-30/P